Making It on a Pastor's Pay

Making It on a Pastor's Pay

Manfred Holck, Jr.

Abingdon Press

Nashville

New York

MAKING IT ON A PASTOR'S PAY

Copyright © 1974 by Abingdon Press

Library of Congress Cataloging in Publication Data

HOLCK, MANFRED, JR.
Making it on a pastor's pay
Bibliography: p.
1. Clergy—Finance, Personal. I. Title.
BV4397.H58   332'.024   73-19105

ISBN-0-687-23034-9

MANUFACTURED BY THE PARTHENON PRESS AT
NASHVILLE, TENNESSEE, UNITED STATES OF AMERICA

To my children
   PETER
   TIMOTHY
   CAROL
   SUSAN
for whom my wife and I
share the responsibilities
of saving and spending
our money

Contents

Chapter
1 What Your Pay Package Is About   11
2 An Earnings–Savings–Spending Plan   19
3 If Your Wife Works   47
4 When You Buy That New Home   60
5 Social Security for Clergymen   82
6 Getting Around by Car   90
7 Investment Ideas for Clergymen   97
8 Retirement Planning—Now   111

Bibliography   125

Introduction

This book is for pastors who are husbands and fathers. Obviously there are pastors other than married males. An increasing number of pastors are female. Some are married; some are not. And there have always been bachelor pastors. But this book is written for the family man, the pastor who shares with a wife and his children the responsibilities for making it on a pastor's pay.

That doesn't mean that female or bachelor pastors won't find some helps here. Of course they will. Very much that is applicable to managing a pastor's money and negotiating for a pay package is common to all pastors. But this book is directed toward a specific group of pastors.

That's because my interest has been in helping families to manage their money, especially the parsonage family where the husband-father is a pastor.

Of course female pastors need help in managing their money more effectively, too. Bachelor pastors have certain unique money problems as well. I suppose I could write a book for each of these groups, too. Perhaps I will someday.

I take responsibility for what has been written here. If there are those who are offended by the male-oriented slant of the contents, my sincere apologies. Certainly no offense has been intended. It is simply my hope that many pastors

9

will find tremendous help in this book toward easing the pain on their beleaguered pocketbooks.

My hearty thanks to all those persons who have commented on various portions of my manuscript and whose helpful suggestions have contributed significantly to any usefulness achieved by this book.

So, read on and may your earnings—savings—spending plan be a successful venture in making it financially on a pastor's pay.

Springfield, Ohio   Manfred Holck, Jr.
January 1974

What Your Pay Package Is About

1

Now there was a time, not so long ago, when a minister was paid $800 a year, given 40 acres to farm, a cow, and such fresh meat, eggs, and vegetables as generous church members might provide. Times have changed, of course, and ministers no longer need to farm and milk, as well as preach, to support their wife and kids.

Yet, a pastor's pay is still not what it ought to be. For many clergymen their salaries are still near the bottom end of the pay scale. In fact ministers are being taken advantage of and imposed upon in a way that congregations should not tolerate.

Far too many congregations have actually failed to take their responsibility seriously. In addition, too many pastors, fearful of antagonizing members or reluctant to express overt concern about money matters, have failed to confide in trusted members about the actual circumstances of their personal financial needs. As a result, congregations have assumed that the pastor's compensation was adequate, while pastors, frustrated in their desire to serve the congregation competently, have fretted about their inability to make ends meet.

Fortunately, many congregational leaders have recently taken significant steps to review their pastor's compensation quite carefully. They have become familiar with the unique income tax benefits applicable to clergymen, many of which are effective only if the congregation takes certain specific advance action. They are aware of the steady and persistent rise in the cost of living and know their pastor is affected as much as they are by constant inflation in food, insurance, transportation, and other costs.

More congregational leaders are also critically evaluating the effectiveness of their pastor's ministry, studying his performance, confidentially discussing with him his personal financial worries, and discovering—for the first time perhaps—what his personal frustrations, ambitions, and goals really are.

Many denominations have taken specific steps to assist congregations in developing helpful procedures for establishing adequate salary levels for their pastors. Among these have been the Guidelines for Clergy Compensation of the Lutheran Church in America. Many congregations have effectively adapted these particular guidelines for their own use. They have learned that failure to do so could possibly lead to serious consequences in their relationship with their pastor.

These guidelines suggest, among other things, what happens to the pastor when his compensation is inadequate:

—discouragement because his family cannot get ahead financially;

—negative attitudes toward his congregation and church;

—inability to meet family and community responsibilities, or participate in continuing education programs;

—necessity to moonlight to make ends meet;

—low retirement plan contributions with resultant inadequate retirement income;

—increased possibility of leaving the ministry;

—difficulty in recruiting men for the ministry;

—and a resulting poor image of the church by the community.

No pastor expects to be wealthy; but for you, me, or anyone else adequate income is necessary for the fulfillment of the responsibilities and obligations you know you should honor.

Sometime during the year your congregation puts together its annual budget. As it puts that new program together, by whatever means, it is particularly critical that serious consideration be given to your compensation. See that it is. With inflation and the cost of everything still spiraling upward at an unprecedented rate, adequate salary increases are imperative for you if you expect your ministry to remain effective. You know all that as well as I do. The important thing is to lift the sights of your members to the point where they recognize your service monetarily in an appropriate way. Your salary, of course, is the base of your pay plan. That's first. Then there's your housing allowance (or parsonage), pension plan arrangements, Social Security allowance, health insurance premiums, vacation time, sick leave benefits, continuing education possibilities, your car allowance, professional expense reimbursements, and a whole host of other matters.

Since your pay package is made up of all those items and perhaps others, it's important that you carefully consider all the factors that influence each item. For example, you'll want to be familiar with income tax rules that affect your pay and allowances, the rate of increase in the cost of living, Social Security effects on clergymen, adequate professional expense reimbursements, vacation time, and continuing education opportunities, plus much more.

Since a clergyman's pay package often includes many items that are not real income, it's important to separate real earnings from payments that are merely reimbursements of professional expenses. Your real income is what you have earned, the wages your congregation has paid you. Reimbursement of professional expenses, such as a car allowance, is simply the congregation's cost of doing business. This is not really part of your pay package.

Yet, for most clergymen, total compensation is often incorrectly calculated to include both earnings and reimbursements for professional expenses. It's important, therefore, that you make the distinction clear to your official board. After all, the congregation's total costs for having a minister, that is the amount included in the budget for all of the expenses associated with paying for a pastor, are not all necessarily income to you. It's not all take-home pay. True, the cost is the same to the congregation either way. But for you, the pastor, it is important that the congregation be aware of your salary—separate and apart—distinct, as it were, from its total cost for having your services. Unless your congregation is aware of the true income they pay you, they'll assume it's a great deal more than it really is. Consequently, you'll only come out on the short end.

An effective way of clarifying this kind of distinction is to list the congregation's expenses related to your services in more than one budget classification. After all, your congregation doesn't list postage under salaries, and benevolences are not a part of office expenses. Neither should car allowances, which are transportation or travel expenses, or mortgage payments on the parsonage, which is debt reduction, be part of salary. These are unrelated to your compensation and should not be shown in the same category as your salary.

Thus, only your base salary and housing allowance should be included in the professional salaries category of your congregational budget. The congregation's payment of pension contributions, health insurance premiums, and other supplemental benefits should be listed as part of professional fringe-benefit costs, along with the costs for providing similar benefits to other employees.

Reimbursements to you for professional expenses should be included among the congregation's operating budget-line expense items. Thus car allowances are, in fact, part of the congregation's travel costs. Postage or supplies you buy are part of the congregation's administrative expenses. Payments on the parsonage mortgage are debt-retirement costs. The distinctions are important.

Your real compensation, therefore, includes only such items as base salary, house allowance, utility allowances, the congregation's contribution to your pension plan, health insurance allowances (or the premiums paid by the congregation for you), Social Security allowances, and such similar items which are strictly compensation to you, real and effective income to you.

The arrangements you have with your congregation on the

various pieces of your compensation package can make a significant difference in your take-home pay. Here are some suggestions that may help boost your pay. In subsequent chapters we'll explain each more fully.

Base salary. Obviously your salary should be fair and equitable. While it should correspond at least with that paid other clergymen with the same responsibilities and experience, a rate closer to that of other professional executives would be more appropriate. Above all, your pay should not be discounted because you elect to spend full time doing the Lord's work or because someone thinks you expect less.

Salary increases. Anything less than a cost-of-living increase is a reduction! Anything more can be considered a merit increase in recognition of fine work you have done.

Housing allowance. If you live in a church-owned house, obviously you don't get an allowance (although you could receive a furnishings allowance). You "pay rent" instead. On the other hand, if you rent or own your home, you should be getting a rental allowance. In either instance, though— parsonage or allowances—you pay no income tax on the rental allowance to the extent it is used to provide a home. Your allowance should be large enough to cover your costs, but not in excess of the fair rental value of your home plus the cost of utilities.

If you actually own your home, you're one up on the renters. On your income tax return you can also deduct the interest and taxes you pay on your home in addition to excluding the allowance from income. Use a sharp pencil to think that one over! That double deduction makes a difference. It adds a little extra to your compensation.

Car allowance. Any professional expense you incur on behalf of your congregation ought to be fully reimbursed to you. That's simply the fair and equitable thing to do. Your congregation should not expect you to finance the legitimate expenses of the church's work out of your own pocket, and you shouldn't volunteer to do so either. The use of your personal automobile on church business is a case in point.

After all, as we have pointed out, this is a legitimate expense of the congregation. It is a cost of doing business. It ought to be paid in full by the congregation. If it's not, talk seriously to some of the businessmen in your congregation about the inequities. Ask them what their own arrangement is where they work. They'll understand your point.

If the church does not or cannot provide a church-owned car for your exclusive use on church business, there are a number of other options possible. Some choices are these:

—a cents-per-mile allowance (10 cents or 12 cents or some other rate). On your tax return you will include the full allowance as income, but deduct 12 cents for the first 15,000 miles you drive on church business, 9 cents thereafter (or deduct actual expenses if they are more). Only time, place, and mileage records required;

—a fixed monthly allowance. Again you include the allowance as income and take the 12 cents–9 cents (or actual expenses) deduction as for the cents-per-mile allowance. In fact, the 12 cents–9 cents deduction is generally available any time if actual expenses are not listed.

In either instance, as we'll point out later, your take-home pay goes up when you can take a tax deduction, such as with the 12 cents–9 cents rule, in excess of your actual costs. You enjoy some tax-free income that way.

Pension plans. If you are in a contributory pension plan (both you and your congregation make a contribution), encourage your congregation to pay the full contribution for you—your contribution as well as that of the congregation. That excludes the entire payment from your present taxable income, thus cutting your income tax some. Besides, as the congregation's contribution goes up each year because of salary advances, the congregation, not you, pays the increase. That's a small built-in salary advance. (If you pay your contribution yourself anyway, look into getting that payment excluded from income through what's called a tax-sheltered annuity arrangement.)

Health insurance. If your congregation pays your health benefit coverage premium for your family, that amounts to a full deduction for tax purposes for you (thus a slight compensation advantage). On the other hand, if you have to pay the premium yourself, you can still get at least a one-half deduction on your tax return (up to $150) when you itemize your deductions, or you get a full deduction if your total medical expenses, including the second half of the premium, exceed 3 percent of your adjusted gross income.

Social Security allowance. Once your congregation has committed itself to providing a Social Security allowance for you that is equal to the maximum tax (your congregation cannot pay the tax for you), they will need to raise the allowance every time the rate goes up—and the rate does keep going up! That's another small built-in salary advance for you even if you do have to pay income tax on the allowance.

Other items. The way in which your congregation handles reimbursements for books and magazine subscriptions, continuing education costs, office supplies, clerical robes, and the like all makes a difference too. In the next several chapters we'll discuss the details of these and other benefits for you.

Your pay package is, of course, very important to you. By doing things correctly as suggested in this and some of the following chapters, you may even be able to avoid paying taxes you don't owe, as well as boost your take-home pay. Avoiding taxes, as we all know, is far different from evading them. The Internal Revenue Service encourages taxpayers to pay only the tax they owe, no more. That's avoiding taxes, not evading them.

Here we have only touched briefly on some of the more important matters you and your congregation will need to consider as your pay package is assembled. In some of the remaining chapters we'll discuss more thoroughly all of these items, plus some others that seriously affect your pocketbook. But in every chapter you'll read about ideas that will help you preserve, protect, and spend your pay better than you do now. It's one thing to earn a salary, and quite another to spend it. In this book we'll not only suggest ways to increase that pay, we'll also try to help you stretch your dollars even more.

You will quickly note that insurance—life, health, property, liability—is not specifically covered in any chapter of this book. The omission is intended. Insurance is such a complex topic that a few pages in this book would serve little useful purpose. A whole book would be required to really tell you what's involved.

Unfortunately there is no full-length book about insurance written specifically for clergymen. However, most of your insurance questions can be answered in other books written for the general public. Your library will have one or more.

Or, your own insurance agent should be able to give you expert guidance. For the best advice your agent should be a full-time insurance salesman and hold a Certified Life Underwriter's certificate.

So, read on to discover what you can do to ease the pinch on your pocketbook.

An Earnings–Savings–Spending Plan
2

Whether you like it or not, you probably have to live within your income. Of course, the purchase of a new car in one year may mean an over expenditure that year (you'll borrow additional funds to make up the difference), but in the following year it means spending less. Certainly in your lifetime you won't be able to spend or use any more than you earn.

As a clergyman, you, like other people, can spend your money for whatever you choose. After all, it is yours to do with as you decide. Your choice is either to spend it or save it. Most people manage to do both; but some, unfortunately, only consume and never save.

To be sure, you have literally hundreds of choices on how to spend and you have many alternatives on how to save or invest. Therefore, a person must constantly make a decision between various alternatives. And certainly, the limited income of a clergyman will never stretch out over all the alternatives available. Your pocketbook just never seems to go far enough. So you set priorities and make choices among the alternatives.

That's precisely what a family budget is supposed to help you do. Businesses use them, and, of course, all levels of government use them as well. While it may take hundreds

19

of staff members to put the federal budget together, only a few minutes a day should take care of your own plan.

A budget, being a financial tool, is like any tool, only as useful as the user makes it. Properly used, it can help you attain your income and spending goals. Ignore it, and you never get out of the woods. Unless you plan carefully all year, you may not, for example, have money available to pay your annual Social Security tax (now over $1,000 a year). A budget can help you.

Your budget is also a financial blueprint of your present and future operations. It is an estimate of what you expect to earn and how you plan to spend. Your budget is a method of planning how you will use your income before you spend it. It's always preceded by a realistic earnings plan.

What's a family budget for? It's to help you manage your personal finances. It's a financial guide to spending that will help you manage your money better than the man without a budget. With a budget, you can make a positive effort to live within your income.

With a budget you'll have to estimate your income, and in the process become acutely conscious of what's available for current needs, and what you'll need for future spending. With a budget you'll learn how to spread your income over all your needs including your savings plan. The process will make you aware of the fact that you really may be saving more than you think through various forced purchases, such as a home or insurance. At any rate, your budget will make perfectly clear to you how much you'll be earning—or at least expect to earn—how much you'll spend, and how much you're really setting aside for future commitments. With a budget you may actually discover alternate ways of spending that produce savings which add to your financial security.

What form should your budget take? It doesn't make a whole lot of difference. Any financial institution will be glad to show you a set of forms they recommend. Or you can make your own. Basically you'll need a listing by day or month down the left side of your record, and columnar headings across the top showing the various categories of income and expenses you've included in your plan.

A budget is more easily planned if it is adjusted to the family's pay period. Since most clergymen are paid on a monthly basis (nothing wrong, of course, with being paid more frequently), a budget of monthly income and outgo would seem the most appropriate. It could also be over any other time span.

Here's a budget plan format that may be useful to you.

Item	Amount
Cash income (after any deductions)	$ _____
Savings:	
Future goals & emergencies	$ _____
Seasonal and/or large expenses	
Regular monthly expenses:	
Mortgage payment (or rent)	$ _____
Utilities	_____
Pension contributions	_____
Installment payments	_____
Other items	_____
Day-to-day expenses:	
Food (including beverages)	$ _____
Household operations	_____
Furnishings	_____
Clothing	_____
Transportation	_____
Medical care	_____
Education, subscriptions	_____
Recreation	_____
Contributions	_____
Personal items	_____
Other items	_____
Total	$ _____

Your budget probably won't be the same as any other family's. But the way you go about putting it together may be quite similar. Here are some general rules that may help you and your family go about the task of putting your family budget together.

1. Establish goals. Your budget must be reasonable and the spending part must certainly be within the limits of income. Be realistic and establish goals that are eventually attainable. Plan for the future. A college education for a child, for example, requires that funds be set aside as early as possible. To do so means other items must be trimmed, perhaps. With a budget you're not as likely to ignore planning for these other future costs.

2. Determine fixed costs. Every clergyman must meet certain fixed commitments, such as a mortgage payment (if he owns his own home) or life insurance premiums. Once those costs are considered (and covered), the variable, nonfixed luxuries and comforts of life can be included.

3. Allocate costs over the year. Funds must be available for those once-a-year insurance premiums (the least expensive way to pay those costs), real estate taxes, college tuition, and similar infrequent payments. Each income period must assume its proportionate share; therefore funds must be set aside and accumulated from each month's pay for them.

4. Cut costs realistically. Not all large expense items are necessarily easy to cut simply because they are large. You'll be tempted to do so, of course, when planned spending exceeds income. It's easier to say you'll cut food costs, for example, on paper, than it is to do it. Your family is likely to spend about the same percentage of its income on food regularly no matter how hard you try to keep costs down. Of course, indiscriminate walking down the grocery aisle will inevitably push your grocery bill way up. Careful shopping will at least keep it consistent.

5. Establish priorities. With a budget you don't need to spell out precisely how you'll spend each penny you earn, but you should develop a set of priorities among the general

items of your expenses. Rules of thumb on various expenditure items are noted throughout this book; yet differing family preferences mean some families spend more on housing or entertainment and less on clothing and education than another family. Set your own priorities, however, based on your own experiences and preferences. This means that though you may not be able to do everything you want, you'll at least know when you can afford what you want to do.

An earnings plan. Every budget begins with income, whether it's a family, a business, or a government agency. You must know what you have to spend before you can plan how to spend it. Normally for clergymen, the primary source of income is in the form of salary from the congregation. Additional income may of course be available from fees, royalties, perhaps interest and dividends, and maybe even real estate rentals. Whatever the source, however, potential income, take-home pay is determined first of all.

Just listing potential income is not the only budget-planning process for available resources. You may want to list potential income in the order of its certainty.

For example, your salary is probably the most certain income your family can expect. Lose your job where you are now, and you'll be out looking in a hurry for another. With the skills you've developed, plus your training and career choice, you'll probably keep earning that same income from month to month without interruption, even if you're forced out of your present church for some reason and move somewhere else.

In cases where your wife works, the income may be less certain. She may intend to pursue a long-term career. Or, her job may be a more or less temporary supplement to the family income. The two of you should seriously evaluate her feelings about her work. Then you can jointly estimate how "certain" the income from it can be counted in your list of potential income.

How "certain" are occasional writing fees, or funeral and wedding fees? They're unpredictable and are not helpful in putting together a specific income budget. They'll be listed as potential income, certainly, to be used for extra desirables but not required expenditures.

Thus, your income budget or resource accumulation list comes in various levels of certainty. List it that way and plan your spending accordingly. It's a much safer way of planning what and when you'll buy.

Your pay. Many people, notably church executives, have written about your salary—how much it ought to be, minimums, average pay, and so forth. Many have diligently tried to raise the sights of church boards, councils, and sessions so that clergymen aren't always the bottom men on the professional pay scale totem pole. Some success has been achieved.

Unfortunately for most clergymen, salary is still at minimum levels, or at least very close to that. All the more reason then that your family budget must be so carefully planned. Your pocketbook is already stretched to its limit. Unless your spending is carefully planned, that pocketbook could be torn to shreds with possible disastrous effects for you, your family, and your career.

There may or may not be rhyme or reason for your pay being at its present level. Someone made a decision, you accepted it, and on that basis you are paid.

Some denominational judicatories have conscientiously developed minimum standards for determining a pastor's pay— and that's more than just setting a minimum for everyone. Clergymen, as in any profession, should receive some recognition for a job well done. Thus, merit increases on top of minimums should be considered. A twenty-year man is normally more qualified than a five-year man (although not necessarily). Responsibilities in a very large church are presumed to be more than in a smaller one. Age and size of congregation may be important factors that require adjustments above any established minimums.

Here's one plan that seems to work well.

1. Salary minimum for senior pastor (80 percent for associates) assuming 1974 dollars.

Years of service	Adult members Up to 300	300–600	600–900	Over 900
Up to 5 years	$ 8,500	$ 9,000	$ 9,500	$10,000
6 to 10 years	10,000	10,500	11,000	11,500
11 to 15 years	11,500	12,000	12,500	13,000
Over 15 years	13,000	13,500	14,000	14,500

2. Free use of a church-owned home or housing allowance equal to at least 25 percent of base salary.
3. Car allowance equal to at least 12 cents a mile.
4. A minimum of 12 percent of salary, housing allowance, and Social Security allowance paid by the congregation to a pension plan.
5. An allowance for Social Security taxes equal to the maximum self-employment Social Security tax applicable each year.
6. A health and death benefit insurance plan, all premiums to be paid by the congregation.
7. At least four weeks vacation.
8. Two additional weeks for continuing education with tuition payments made by the congregation.
9. A three-month sabbatical each six years of service with the same congregation.
10. And, full reimbursement for all professional expenses.

Another plan proposes the following arrangement: Beginning the first year in the ministry, basic salary is proposed at $100 a week, increasing by $5 a week for each year in the ministry. Reimbursement for automobile expenses is set at $35 a week, including the cost of replacement. A provision for various state, federal, and Social Security taxes suggests $35 a week with a $1 per week increase for each year in the ministry.

The pastor is, of course, provided with a parsonage and utilities or a housing allowance to cover both (assumed at 25 percent of base salary value). A weekly pension allowance of $15 plus disability insurance coverage is suggested. A book and study-material allowance is also recommended for which $100 a year is anticipated.

If your congregation followed that pattern, the cost to the congregation would be something like this:

	1st year	10th year	20th year	30th year
Base salary	$ 5,200	$ 7,800	$10,400	$13,000
Automobile allowance	1,820	1,820	1,820	1,820
Tax allowance	1,820	2,340	2,860	3,380
Pension plan	780	1,300	1,820	2,340
Health insurance, etc.	312	468	624	780
Book & study material	100	100	100	100
Parsonage/housing	1,300	1,950	2,600	3,250
Total cost to church	$11,332	$15,778	$20,224	$24,670

On the other hand, that would not all be income to the pastor either. Here is a schedule showing the real income, fringe benefits, and expense reimbursements in this situation. Divided this way, the pastor's net take-home pay would be much less than the congregation's total cost for having a pastor.

Real income:				
Base salary	$ 5,200	$ 7,800	$10,400	$13,000
Tax allowance	1,820	2,340	2,860	3,380
Parsonage/housing	1,300	1,950	2,600	3,250
Net take-home pay	$ 8,320	$12,090	$15,860	$19,630
Fringe benefits:				
Pension plan	$ 780	$ 1,300	$ 1,820	$ 2,340
Health insurance, etc.	312	468	624	780
Book & study material	100	100	100	100
	$ 1,192	$ 1,868	$ 2,544	$ 3,220
Reimbursements:				
Automobile allowance	$ 1,820	$ 1,820	$ 1,820	$ 1,820
Total cost to church	$11,332	$15,778	$20,224	$24,670

It's obvious that take-home pay and the congregation's expense for having a pastor are not the same thing. This distinction is important.

If you are interested in the arrangements that are possible for a sabbatical program for yourself, here's one developed by St. Martin's Lutheran Church, Austin, Texas for its pastors. It has merit.

1. Definition: Pastoral sabbatical is leave of absence for self-betterment to further service in God's kingdom.

2. Six years of service at this church will be required before a leave is considered.

3. Leave not to exceed one year.

4. Replacement arrangements to be negotiated between the pastors and the church council.

5. A minimum of one year between staff sabbaticals will be required.

6. Financial support by this congregation.
   a. Base salary
   b. Housing allowance
   c. Pension payments
   d. Insurance premiums
        (a, b, c, d to be frozen for duration of leave)
   e. Tuition costs and fees
   f. Mileage allowance to and from location of study
   Any stipends or scholarships awarded to pastor to be deducted from this support package.

7. All continuing education time and monies available to be used as part of the leave.

8. Vacation and continuing education provisions may not be accrued during sabbatical.

9. This policy is to be administered by the church council.

10. Any other arrangements not covered by these policies shall be the responsibility of the church council.

*Tax planning tips.** The old cliché that only two things in life are inevitable, death and taxes, is as true for ministers as for anyone else. It may be that a clergyman has some deeper insight into the meaning and mystery of the first and little about the other, at least more so, in that order, than a professional tax accountant. But he, like the accountant who is also

* Adapted from "Tax Planning for Clergymen," *Tax Ideas* by Manfred Holck, Jr. (Englewood Cliffs, N.J.: Prentice-Hall), 1973.

affected by both, will do well to prepare for the inevitable, and learn as much as he can about them before either day dawns—April 15, to be specific, for income tax, date unknown for the other.

Putting together a pastor's pay package also involves the consideration of several income tax matters. The proper combination of salary and benefits can often reduce a clergyman's tax bill with very little or no additional cost to the congregation.

I could, of course, write a whole book on the clergyman's income taxes—it has been done. But that's not the purpose of this book. I have only noted some special cases which seem most useful to ministers. If you need help or have particular problems with completing your income tax return, I suggest you check these titles (see Bibliography):

Clergy's Federal Income Tax Guide
Your Federal Income Tax
Your Income Tax
The Minister's Income Tax

Example: Amounts spent by a minister to provide a home in excess of a rental allowance are not deductible. *Action:* Have the congregation agree on a total amount of compensation for salary and rental allowance combined, permitting the clergyman to specify within IRS limits that portion of the total to be designated as allowance. Too much allowance is better than not enough. *Result:* No additional cost to the congregation but possible significant additional income exclusions and tax savings to the clergymen.

Example: If the church owns the parsonage but the minister must purchase his own furniture and pay for his own utilities, only the rental value of the home is excluded from income. He'll pay tax on the income used to buy that furniture and pay the heat bill. *Action:* Designate a portion of the minister's base salary for rental allowance not to exceed the rental value of furnishings and cost of utilities. *Result:* The minister can then exclude from income any allowance used to buy furniture or pay utilities. It cuts the minister's tax bill, yet costs the congregation nothing.

Example: Contributions made to a qualified pension plan can be excluded from taxable income only through a salary reduction plan. *Action:* Be certain the minister and congregation are contributing to an approved plan. Reduce the minister's salary by his contribution and have the congregation pay the entire amount. *Result:* A cut in the minister's tax at no cost to the congregation.

Example: Health insurance premiums paid by a minister are deductible only if the minister itemizes deductions, and then only one-half is included (up to $150) unless medical expenses exceed 3 percent of adjusted gross income when the whole premium is included. *Action:* Have the congregation pay the entire premium by designating that amount as a special allowance. *Result:* A full deduction, in effect, for the pastor for that premium payment whether or not he itemizes deductions. If salary is reduced for this amount, there is no extra cost to the congregation. Of course, it would be much better for the congregation to pay that full premium anyway without reducing salary. It's still not taxable income to the minister and there's only a nominal increase in total congregational costs.

Example: Group term life insurance premiums paid by the minister cannot be deducted. *Action:* Have the congregation pay those premium costs, along with the health insurance premiums in the same way. *Result:* More tax-free income to the minister.

Example: Social Security self-employment taxes keep going up, and ministers (as well as other self-employeds) are digging deeper than ever into their pockets to pay the premiums. *Action:* Have the congregation designate an allowance for Social Security equal each year to the maximum self-employment Social Security tax. *Result:* The minister's take-home pay remains unchanged as the tax goes up. Any increases in costs can be absorbed more readily by the congregation. It's a small built-in salary advance each year for the minister. (The allowance must be paid to the minister, and it is taxable income to him. The congregation cannot pay the tax for him.)

Example: A minister normally spends more to operate his car than he receives in reimbursement. Of course, he can deduct the excess costs, but all the same, he's cutting into his already meager salary to pay those extra costs. *Action:* Provide a car with all expenses paid for the minister's exclusive use on church business. *Result:* The minister's pay is not reduced by excess costs coming out of his pocketbook, and the congregation is doing what is fair by reimbursing the minister in full for his church-related professional expenses. The minister can then ignore the whole matter for tax purposes.

Example: Every clergyman has professional expenses (in addition to his automobile), such as books, magazines, tape-recording equipment, pulpit robes, professional dues, home entertainment of church guests, and so forth. All these expenses are tax deductible; nevertheless, they are expenses—out-of-pocket cost. *Action:* Have the congregation provide full reimbursement for all professional expenses. *Result:* The congregation pays the proper costs for having a minister, and the minister ignores the matter for tax purposes. (Of course, the minister had better keep good records anyway, so he can request full reimbursement.)

Example: Many ministers participate in continuing education opportunities to improve their skills. But that costs money. Of course it is usually deductible, but it is still another expense, another drain on the minister's resources. *Action:* Have the congregation pay all or part of those costs. After all, it's for their benefit. *Result:* It may cost the congregation something more, but it relieves the minister's paying, and eliminates any possible tax question concerning the legality of the claimed deduction.

Example: Most congregations offer their ministers a fixed monthly automobile allowance. Ministers may deduct their actual costs or 12 cents a mile up to 15,000 miles, 9 cents a mile thereafter. Yet the allowance is artificially fixed, and often has no bearing on costs for operating a car in that community. *Action:* Have the congregation pay a mileage allowance (10 cents a mile minimum). *Result:* The allowance is geared to miles driven and thus more nearly to costs incurred. The 12 cents–9 cents deduction (or actual costs) is still applicable. The congregation probably won't pay much more allowance than by the old way. At any rate, it will be a much fairer reimbursement plan.

Your spending plan. Expenditures are the other side of that budget coin—some are major items, like a house or an automobile, others quite minor, like rubber bands and paper clips. Some are must items over which you really have very little control: your mortgage payments, insurance premiums and Social Security taxes. To be sure, you could sell your home to buy a less expensive one, cancel your insurance or at least reduce coverage, and you might be successful in applying for exemption from Social Security if the deadline hasn't already gone by you. But normally, items such as these are fixed, at least for the short run.

Food, clothing, entertainment, and travel, however, are all costs that can be controlled to a certain extent. It's difficult to cut food costs, as we noted previously, but wise shopping and the purchase of less expensive grades of foods offers an opportunity to cut costs.

Different families spend different amounts on similar items. This happens because of family sizes, likes and dislikes, or simply a different set of priorities. Some families will eat out often, others never. One family prefers a hearty and different breakfast each day, in another it's everyone for himself. The wardrobes in some families may be smaller with more spent on luxury and prepackaged foods. Others may splurge on clothing, spend less on foods. It all depends. Our priorities are at least partly personal. A comparison of your budget with an average budget may, therefore, really not be meaningful at all.

You'll run into budget problems when you pay insurance premiums annually (even though that is the least expensive way), as item 3 under the general rules for budgeting notes. An equal amount set aside each month solves that problem and provides the funds when the premium comes due. Budgeting is simple then.

Here's how one family handles their funding of those annual premiums.

There are three life insurance policies on which I pay annual premiums. Compare the savings.*

Amount of Policy	Type	Life Insured	12 Months Cost Annual Premium	Monthly Premium	Annual Premium Savings	Percentage Savings
$20,000	Term	Husband	$215.20	$228.00	$ 12.80	5.9
7,000	Straight	Wife	182.10	194.40	12.30	6.7
5,000	Straight	Husband	107.70	117.00	9.30	8.6

My other policies probably work out at about the same savings. But on these three policies alone, by paying once a year, I save $34.40 on $32,000 coverage. I consider the potential savings important enough to make an extra effort to achieve it.

The same savings accrue on health insurance premiums. My family policy with a one-time annual premium cost is $275. Quarterly it costs $286 a year. I save $11 annually by paying once a year.

It's one thing to want to pay an annual premium; it's another thing to do it. Here's how I try. At the beginning of each year I figure out what I'll need to pay in annual premiums during the next twelve months and the due dates involved. For the three life policies and health policy listed above, my annual premium cost is $780. That's $65 a month. So I budget that amount each month.

I not only budget for it; I actually set it aside. When that $275 health insurance comes due (or any of the other premiums for that matter), I'd never have enough cash to pay it all out in one month, even with a budget. So, I actually set the cash aside. In my checkbook I keep three funds going, as if I had three checking accounts. One fund is my regular fund, another is for insurance premiums, the third

* Manfred Holck, Jr., editor, *Church and Clergy Finance*, Vol. 2, No. 23 (Springfield, Ohio: January 5, 1972).

for contributions (I pay some contributions annually). Then, each month I take $65 out of the regular fund, and put it into the insurance fund.

The cash is still all in the same checking account, but I know I can't spend any more than my regular fund balance in order to have enough for insurance costs later on. If I overspend the regular fund, I surely won't be able to pay insurance premiums when they are due. The increasing fund, then, will always have the cash I need to pay annual premiums when they are due.

The first time such a funding effort is set up, an initial transfer in excess of $65 would be necessary. For example: The cash required to pay the premiums on those four policies looks like this—$215.20 in February, $182.10 in September, $107.70 in October, and $275.00 in December. The fund would need $85.20 at the beginning of the year to make the plan work. After the first year it should carry itself along, unless premiums change or other policies are added.

Month	Required	Transfer	Balance
Initial Payment		$ 85.20	$ 85.20
January	-0-	65.00	150.20
February	$215.20	65.00	-0-
March	-0-	65.00	65.00
April	-0-	65.00	130.00
May	-0-	65.00	195.00
June	-0-	65.00	260.00
July	-0-	65.00	325.00
August	-0-	65.00	390.00
September	182.10	65.00	272.90
October	102.70	65.00	230.20
November	-0-	65.00	295.20
December	275.00	65.00	85.20
January	-0-	65.00	150.20
February	215.20	65.00	-0-
March	-0-	65.00	65.00
April	-0-	65.00	130.00

You may not need that kind of separate fund to be sure you have the cash on hand to pay your annual premiums when they are due. I need the discipline, though, and it has worked well for me. This is a way in which I save at least 6 percent of the cost of insurance premiums each year. If you need a money-saving technique, why not try this plan for yourself?

Here, then, are some average spending plans that may be helpful to you in your own budget planning.

A Guide to Budgeting for the Young Couple, published by the USDA, suggests family spending for incomes above and below $5,000 like this:

	Lower Income Percent	Higher Income Percent
Total money income	100	100
Total for current living	83	80
Food & beverages	19	18
Shelter (rent, etc.)	13	12
Fuel & utilities	4	4
Household operations	5	5
Furnishings & equipment	5	4
Clothing	8	7
Transportation	15	16
Medical care	5	5
Recreation & education	5	5
Personal & miscellaneous	4	4
Gifts and contributions	3	3
Personal insurance	4	4
Income taxes	10	12
Savings	0	1

Your spending plan may not look anything like either of these. As was pointed out, expenditures vary from family to family because of differences in family sizes, tastes, priorities, and such individual preferences. Even your age and that

of your children will make a difference in how much you
spend in any particular category.
Young families just getting started have different needs
than the couple about to retire. If you have children in college, you know your expenditures are far different than when
they were in grade school. Once they are out of the family
nest, your costs change again. So, your budget is a personal,
flexible, changing thing. You'll do well to remember to keep
it that way as you plan priorities and make commitments.

In 1971 the Bureau of Labor Statistics suggested that a family
of four requires the following amounts to live on. Remember,
though, that inflation has probably added about 15 per cent to
these amounts.

	Lower Budget		Moderate Budget		Higher Budget	
Food	$1,778	27%	$ 2,288	23%	$ 2,821	19%
Housing	1,384	21%	2,351	23%	3,544	24%
Transportation	484	7%	940	9%	1,215	8%
Clothing & personal care	780	12%	1,095	11%	1,609	11%
Medical care	539	8%	543	5%	565	4%
Other family consumption *	320	5%	601	6%	1,050	7%
Personal taxes	619	10%	1,348	14%	2,523	18%
Other costs **	663	10%	911	9%	1,262	9%
Total budget	$6,567		$10,077		$14,589	

* Includes reading materials, recreation, education, tobacco, alcoholic bever-
    ages, and such miscellaneous things as bank service charges, legal fees,
    and children's allowances.
** Includes allowances for gifts and contributions, life insurance, occupational
    expense, Social Security, and other non-income taxes.

Take all this information and use it as a guide to put together your own program based on your own resources,
needs, commitments, and wants. Here is a procedure that
may be helpful.
You can begin your own plan by finding out where you've
been. Set up a columnar listing with headings similar to
those shown on the Earnings—Savings—Spending Plan

Worksheet; or use a separate sheet of paper for each category. Go back through all your spending records for the last
twelve months and write down where your money has gone.
Sort out check stubs, receipts, cash payment books, tax records, anything that lists what you've spent. You'll catch almost
everything that way. It's not an easy job, but to get an accurate picture you must do it. (If your records are incom-
plete, your best "guesstimate" will have to do.)

Total your figures. Now, for the first time in your life
perhaps, you have a clear picture of what it's costing you for
food or for transportation or clothing or anything else. With
that information in hand, you're ready to plan your earnings—savings—spending for the next twelve months.

There's one important decision, though, before you set
down proposed spending. Have a family conference to set
goals and objectives for what you want. Of course you want
enough to live comfortably, but what are some of your long-
range needs or wants—your big plans: a college education
for the children, a down payment on a house, a new car,
a special trip. Maybe there are smaller things you'll want,
too—new curtains, a bookshelf, a bicycle. Put them down
under special wants. These are the things you can save for
once you have your emergency savings plan up to par.

If you have outstanding debts (not including your house
payments or rent), develop a plan to pay them off. Once
paid, continue the same payments into your savings plan.

Now look over those expenses for the past twelve months.
Have they been realistic? Is one category all out of propor-
tion over others? Can you stick to these limits next year?
What can you cut to add to savings? To be sure, it's not
an easy task to put things together, but to do so means you
will spend more intelligently and wisely in the months
ahead.

If as you plan, and no matter how hard you try, your
savings—spending continue to go over your income, you'll
have to cut somewhere. But if cuts are called for—and they
probably are—make them. If they're needed to keep income
and expense equal, they were obviously needed long before

this. As painful as it may be, there's no better time than now to face the facts head on. You may simply have to spend less, as impossible as that may seem.

If all else fails to bring expense (including your savings plan contributions) and income into balance, you can always lump some of your variable costs together. Take clothing, medical, and personal allowances together. If everyone stays well, you get new clothes; if not, you stick to absolute necessities. If wardrobes will really do for another year, everyone gets a personal allowance to do with as he or she wants; if not, the allowance goes.

In any listing be sure you include all appropriate costs. That way you'll know how much it's costing you for housing or running your car. Utilities are part of housing costs; so are your homeowner's insurance, maintenance, and household help. Car expenses include the obvious—gas, oil, insurance, tires, and the like—but also your monthly payments, or if you paid cash, the amount you're setting aside for the next car.

Once all has been agreed upon, balanced, and entered on your worksheet (annual and monthly), you're ready for business. Each month as you total up costs for those thirty days, enter them on your worksheet, and then compare. Compare what you said you would do with what you did. If there are variances, find out what went wrong. Maybe you'll need to change your plans. After all, the plan outlined below is a guide, not a rigid rule. It can be changed in midstream to meet new or unexpected conditions.

Once tried, you'll find that it really works. You know what you've got; you know what you've spent. There's no better way to plan your spending. Either the money is there, or it isn't. The difference is that this way you know what you've got to work with, how you used it, and what you can do with it next month.

There are many specific ways in which clergymen can cut costs, sometimes rather dramatically. Your earnings—savings —spending plan sets the parameters. But within those limits you can move around a good deal getting the most for each

dollar you spend, stretching that pocketbook to make your
money buy more for less.

EARNINGS—SAVINGS—SPENDING PLAN

	Annual Plan	Monthly Plan	First Month Actual	Second Month Actual	Third Month Actual
EARNINGS—					
Salary					
Allowances:					
Housing					
Car					
Other					
Honoraria					
Other income					
Total income					
SAVINGS—					
Emergency					
Big plans					
Special plans					
Investment plan					
SPENDING—					
Church/charities					
Food					
Professional:					
Dues					
Subscriptions					
Books/supplies					
Automobile:					
Cost					

Insurance	
Gas, oil	
Tires, repairs	
Education:	
Continuing	
Children	
Music, special	
Housing:	
Rent/payments	
Insurance	
Taxes	
Utilities	
Furnishings	
Maintenance	
Operations	
Life insurance	
Clothing	
Medical:	
Insurance	
Hospital	
Drugs	
Doctors	
Personal allowances	
Recreation	
Vacation	
Gifts	
Miscellaneous	

Total Savings—Special—Spending

It's no secret that good personal money management is essentially the business of doing sensible things with your money. Careless grocery shopping, unlimited use of a charge plate, random scurrying around in a car, and indiscriminate book buying are obviously not sensible ways to manage your money.

To spend money simply because at that precise moment you think you need, want, or must have an item is poor planning, poor management, and a wasteful use of your personal resources. Your clergyman's paycheck is limited enough. The way you spend the little you have, therefore, is extremely important. Obviously, you must do sensible things with your money if you ever expect to keep your head above water and your personal finances solvent.

These days it's sink or swim. So you'd best find ways to stay afloat. Here are some randomly selected, specific suggestions on cutting expenses and saving.

—Avoid charge accounts that require a service fee. Charge all you want, pay in the required time (normally thirty days) if you can, but don't delay beyond the time when a service charge adds cost. If you tarry, it can cost you as much as 18 percent interest annually.

—Avoid a dime-a-time checking account, unless you write less than fifteen checks a month. The service charge on regular checking accounts is normally less expensive. And some regular accounts are now free. Shop around.

—Walk whenever you can. It's certainly cheaper and healthier, too. Avoid the temptation to go only five blocks by car.

—Shop around for prescriptions. Brand name items sell at different prices at different stores in the same neighborhood. Prescriptions written for drugs are usually cheaper (often by many times) than prescriptions written for brand names.

—Don't be proud about where you get your clothing. Buy used clothing, good older furniture at thrift stores. There are bargains there.

—For real bargains, attend an auction of household goods, but be careful. Know what top prices you'll pay before you bid and then don't go over.

—For inexpensive Christmas wrapping, use outdated wallpaper sample books from your local paint store. It's perfectly good paper, and colorful, too.

—Traveler's checks are OK, but avoid buying them if you can charge most things on a trip. Use a credit card when you can. It eliminates that 1 percent cost for checks—but don't lose the cards and don't delay paying that charge when your bill comes due.

—Limit your deductible collision insurance coverage on your car to the maximum you consider desirable. By raising the deductible coverage enough you may cut your cost by half. Even on new cars, most people can reasonably afford to pay the first $100 or $200 damage cost. Insurance costs should go for the large damages and losses. On old cars especially, collision insurance is not worth the cost.

—Put your savings where they will be safe and earn the greatest return—in a savings and loan association, not a bank.

—If you live close to a public or college library, encourage them to carry subscriptions to the magazines you read. Then cancel your own.

—Pack a lunch if you're off on an all day member-visiting jaunt. A ham sandwich on rye with chips and a thermos of tea is at least one-fourth the cost you'll pay at the local drive-in.

—Don't buy the first edition of every new book. Wait and check the discount and paperback book list first. Visit used book stores. For free books use your library privileges.

—Use photocopy machines sparingly. They're tempting, but costs skyrocket. You got along without them once; save money now. Use them less.

—Stay away from installment loans, if you can. Pay cash, but if you must borrow, the local bank will probably offer the best rate.

—Taking a long trip by car? Plan carefully. Leave early (4:00 a.m.), pack a light breakfast and a picnic lunch for the first two meals. Saves time and money.

—Need to borrow money? Check the cash or loan value of your life insurance policies. At 5 percent or 6 percent that will be the cheapest money you can find.

—Try term life insurance. It's cheap for the coverage, much cheaper than any other kind of life insurance. There are drawbacks, though. Check with your insurance agent.

—If you're a full service customer at your local bank, you'll get preferential treatment on loan rates and a lot of free service and advice besides. Slightly reduced earnings on savings accounts may be worth the other extra services. Explore the possibilities.

—Buy whole chickens and cut them yourself. The price per pound is less. Of course, chicken is a good buy almost anytime.

—Time grocery shopping. Every minute the shopper stays after half an hour costs another 50 cents, so the supermarket managers figure.

—Is your parsonage or manse big, with lots of storage space? Try buying food and household items in large lots. Canned goods and dry goods may be cheaper that way.

—Extra-life light bulbs aren't always a bargain. They last longer, but use more electricity.

—Use regular or low-lead gasoline. Shun the cars that require special gas. Figure your miles per gallon both ways. Could save you $50 a year.

—Learn the bus routes in your town. Beats the price of a taxi. Probably cheaper than a car, too, if you're going more than three miles.

—There's nothing wrong with trading stamps. Take all you can get and cash them in on merchandise you want or need. Double check the stores you patronize; their prices could be higher than the nonstamp stores.

—Plan ahead. Buy when the market's right for what you need and not just when you happen to want an item, i.e., buy storm windows in June, next year's Christmas cards, decorations and wrappings after Christmas Day, camping trailers in September, swimming equipment at the end of the summer, snow sleds in spring.

—Get a hair-clipping set and cut your son's hair. Saves money. A few times doing it yourself will more than pay for the clippers. Have yours cut at home too. It could save you more than $50 a year! You can also very quickly learn to give your wife a trim to cut down on her beauty parlor expenses.

—Clothes sewn at home will, in a short time, more than pay for the cost of sewing lessons and a machine. A home-sewn robe and surplice (for those clergymen who wear them) could be 60 percent less expensive, and just as good!

—Those self-operated dry cleaning machines are money-savers, and the results are almost as good as when done professionally.

—Home-delivery milk is usually more expensive than cartons bought in the grocery store. Gallons are normally cheaper than two half-gallons. Quality is important, of course, and many brands are good, safe, and adequate. Also, use powdered milk in cooking or mixed with whole milk for drinking.

—Thinking about another cross-country vacation this year? You may want to skip it this once. Save the money, stay at home. See the sights right in your own hometown, county, or nearby city. It's far less expensive, for sure, and may turn out to be just as enjoyable, if not more so.·

—Grocery shop once a week. Go with a list in hand, but keep it flexible. Shop the same stores regularly as you become familiar with what's a bargain and what's a come-on.

—Keep a sharp lookout for good sales. Maybe they are only a come-on, but there's no reason not to buy if you need the item. Just don't buy what you don't need, even if it is on sale.

—Take in all the free entertainment you can find. Watch for your favorite movies to appear on TV. Summer park concerts, usually free, are fun for the whole family. Museums, art exhibits, and a whole host of other places can provide days of inexpensive fun.

—Sell your second car. Ride a bicycle (yes, even when making calls on members!), walk, or take the bus.

—Grow your own salads and vegetables. A ten-foot-square plot can grow a lot of fresh food. Even if the church does own the yard, who can really object?

—By the time your children are sixteen, they should be earning their own spending money. Insist they do.

—Search every possibility for scholarships for your college-bound kids. Write for information. Don't overlook the possibilities of low-rate educational loans if the search for grants doesn't pan out. You'll pay back a cheaper dollar as inflation offsets the interest costs.

—Dial direct. Avoid operator assisted long-distance telephone calls. Better yet, plan to write more often.

—Avoid extension phones, plug-in jacks, color phones, and fancy models in your home. Stick to the plain black model. It's the least expensive arrangement and works just as well.

—Don't pay off the mortgage on your home ahead of time. With inflation soaring you're paying a cheaper dollar every month.

—Turn off the TV when you leave the room. Do the same with lights. It may save only pennies, but it bolsters your money-saving resolve.

—In winter, turn down the thermostat. Day-time winter heat at 70 degrees is comfortable. At night, turn it down even more. Whether you or your church pays the bill, you will soon notice the difference in heat costs.

—Start on your Christmas presents during the summer. Make them, or if you buy, do that too, in the summer months. Avoid the rush and high prices of December days.

—You need exercise, but you don't need all the exercise paraphernalia. Walk, jog, bicycle, swim, or do something else. Membership in the local YMCA should be explored.

—Impulse buying is expensive. Keep a running list of what you need. Write now and pay later.

—Wash your own car. Mow your own lawn.

If after all that, you still can't make ends meet, there is yet another possibility. Maybe you can boost your income some. Have you tried submitting a good sermon manuscript or an article to a magazine publisher? Most pay at least a nominal amount upon publication. Try a garage sale. If your family is at all typical, you've got a lot of things around the house you don't use any more. Someone may be willing to pay for them.

Peddle your services as an after-dinner speaker. Try teaching a course in your local community college. Is your wife handy at the sewing machine? Maybe a friend will pay to have a dress custom made. Should your wife work at outside employment, full time or even part time?

Even if you can move the income dollars up, you may really need to cut spending, too. I know, that's easier said than done. When you think it over you can probably discover a number of places where some drastic changes are not only possible but desirable. Work at it, you'll find something that can go.

Finally. You can keep your family budget solvent. I've suggested some ways in this chapter. Now it's up to you and your family. In summary, here's the way you go about the task.

1. Keep reasonable records. Know where your money comes from and where it goes. A simple notebook record will do. Don't worry about all the pennies, just be sure the dollars are accounted for.

List your annual income, prorated monthly. List your unavoidable expenses—rent, taxes, savings. Take the difference and juggle your day-to-day expenses to get the most for your money left over. A few months trial basis will soon tell you where you're over-spending or mis-spending. Your notebook record, month by month, will soon become a real key to a successful spending plan.

2. Make your savings an unavoidable expense. Each payday, before you spend a dime on anything else, sock away something for your rainy day fund. Your emergency savings plan goal should be up to four months salary or more. That's your nest egg, your cushion, your comfort when financial emergencies hit. It won't be there, it won't grow, unless you make it happen that way.

3. Set reasonable limits on your spending plan, then change them if they don't work. Your total must obviously be within your income, but don't squeeze individual items unnecessarily

if you can't possibly meet your goal. Trade off for something else. After all, you can't normally anticipate accidents and illness. You'll have an emergency car-repair bill, too, from time to time. Switch around, keep flexible.

4. Put the entire family to work on planning your spending. Bring the children into the process. Let everyone help. You'll be amazed how well that can work. If everyone knows the family's financial goals, each one will work to achieve them.

5. Give everyone a personal allowance—yourself and your spouse as well. Don't ask for an account record. Let everyone spend that money any way he pleases. Children fast become adept at handling money when given the chance to use it. They'll probably squander less than you. If your wife wants to spend her share on an extra fancy dress, fine. Maybe you'll have a night out with friends (or your wife!). For it's that kind of free money that does wonders for family morale.

6. If all else fails, cut your spending or raise your income. If you can't make ends meet and you're living beyond your means, you might as well face it. Only you can do anything about it.

If Your Wife Works
3

Should your wife work? Well, that all depends. The Department of Labor reports over 18 million working wives, and the number is growing. Wives of many clergymen work, and most congregations hardly give the matter a second thought. But does a working wife add much money to the family coffers? That may be the key to the question whether or not your wife should work.

If your wife does work, it's probably for a good reason. You may simply need more money. Perhaps your church doesn't pay enough, or you have a youngster in college. Your wife may have skills and training that are useful and needed and she may enjoy exercising them. If you have children at home, it may be a case of necessity that makes your wife bring home a second paycheck. An older wife with no one at home anymore might work for the pleasure of being useful.

But does that second paycheck automatically mean that your income is going up? Not necessarily so. In fact, you may only be breaking even. Maybe it's even costing more than she makes. This is all a warning for the two of you to carefully consider the decision as to whether she should work or not. You will both need to calculate carefully all those extra costs incurred because she is working—extra deductions, dues, and taxes that will come off the top of her pay. In fact, the two of you may decide to look around instead to see how effective just cutting costs at home would be. It may be you and your wife may decide that you will save more dollars by not holding down an outside job than if she is working each day from 8 o'clock to 5 o'clock, making her weekly cash contribution to your beleaguered bank account.

Check it out. You and your wife may find far more expenses—both obvious and hidden—related to her working than you may have bargained for. Here are some of them—you may think of others.

For example, there are the ever-present and ominous payroll deductions, many of which don't affect your take-home pay from your church at all, but will affect your wife's.

Your wife will pay Social Security taxes right off the bat, and that is 5.8 percent of her wages to begin with. Of course, you as a clergyman pay that tax, too, at an even higher rate. Don't forget that almost 6 percent of your wife's pay goes for a tax she may never be able to utilize, unless she works long enough and earns enough. That is because she already has Social Security protection since you are covered. When you die or retire, she will have a choice of taking her Social Security benefits under your participation, or because of her own rights. For most wives, chances are their own benefits will be less than what they get through their husband's share. It's a tax she'll pay, but from which she may never gain any benefits.

She will, of course have income taxes withheld. That will lower her take-home pay, but she'll get some back if it is too much. However, you will jointly pay more income tax anyway—at least if your own income is enough so you owe a tax on it alone. You can figure that at least 14 percent of her income goes for income tax (that's the minimum rate). If you're in a higher tax bracket, a greater share, maybe 20 percent, will go for income taxes. That is because any income you or she earn on top of your basic salary simply adds to your taxable income. So that's more income she won't ever see.

Most people now live in areas that have local income taxes —city, county, or state. Figure another 2 percent to 5 percent for that. If Workmen's Compensation or Unemployment Taxes are withheld from salaries in your state, you can count on a few more pennies dropped from each hour of work.

If your wife works for a union-shop organization, she'll pay union dues. Not much each month perhaps, but don't forget to include that cost in your calculations. It's a cost for which your working wife may not get much benefit. She may not even have a choice in the matter.

Most employers have group life, health, and accident insurance plans. Premium costs may be paid in full, in part, or not at all by either employer or employee. They may or may not be voluntary plans. So your working wife could be stuck with premiums for insurance plans she doesn't need.

Your wife's group life insurance might be useful (though it's probably term, which is all right), and is applicable only so long as she works for that employer. You do need some insurance on your wife's life, but it ought to be more permanent and you need it whether or not your wife is working for this particular employer. Again, it's a benefit that she may have to pay for, but one you probably don't need.

Your own family insurance plan should include health and accident insurance coverage for you and every member of your family. That's only a sensible and reasonable thing to do. However, if your wife works, she will probably be required to participate in a health plan, and may have to pay the premiums, too. While it may be desirable coverage for her, don't fool yourself into thinking you will get double reimbursement if she is flat on her back in a hospital bed. You may get full reimbursement so her stay won't cost you anything, but the family policy you hold which covers her, plus her own policy, are not likely to pay more than your actual costs.

That's because both policies probably have what's called a coordination-of-benefits clause attached to each, which means that if more than one policy is involved in a claim, the insurance companies will coordinate benefits in such a way that you are reimbursed for no more than your total costs. So, the extra premium your wife has to pay for coverage on herself could be expensive for the amount of benefit that might accrue under that policy. It's another cost that cuts take-home pay. How much? Check it out with a prospective employer.

Contributions to a pension plan may be required of all employees where your wife expects to work. That could lop another 10 percent off that gross pay. Depending on the plan involved, she may or may not get that money back (if so, there's no telling when, perhaps when she quits, maybe not until she is sixty-five). A vested plan assures her at least someday of getting something back. But, a deduction now from gross pay cuts down on what she will bring home this week to help pay for groceries. It is another cost that may not be of much benefit to you now, or ever.

Besides that, there could be other deductions, too. Along with all the other employees, your wife could be expected to agree to a payroll withholding for the local United Fund campaign, the Boy Scout Capital Fund-raising effort, or no telling what else. Another cost, another cut, another drain.

All these deductions may very well give you and your family some greater security. Still, with less costs you may be able to provide the same benefits out of your own pay for your wife, kids, and yourself. If your wife works, however, you will pay extra for them.

If you have children, especially smaller ones, a working wife means child-care costs, either with a baby-sitter at home or elsewhere. Preschool children especially will cost, but even those in school need some care after school is out, not to mention school holidays and summer vacations. Perhaps your schedule is flexible enough—and your congregation doesn't mind—so that you can care for the kids part of the day at home. That will cut costs, to be sure, but it may also hamper your work. Better weigh the alternatives.

You get a tax break on child-care costs if your wife works full time. You can actually deduct up to $4,800 during the year, with some limitations, for those costs. That might cut your taxes by some $700, but, of course, you shelled out $4,800 from the money your wife is earning to pay for child care.

It may not leave very much of what she has earned in the end. A job very far from your home means extra transportation costs for your wife, there and back. If that involves a second car there will be a drastic surge in travel costs. At the very least, a job too far to walk to means bus fare every day. Even if your scheduling does let both of you use one car, there will be times when it is simply inconvenient or impossible—you are out of town, there is a hospital call or funeral, you name it. (The name of the game is often "emergency" when you are dealing with all the potential unknown problems of ministering to a church full of members.) The point is, don't overlook the possible conflict in transportation if you think you will keep costs down because you plan to use one car for the both of you.

There are other costs your wife will face once on the job. Unless she carries a lunch she will buy, which is always more costly than eating at home. Coffee breaks require 10 cents or 20 cents a time (twice a day, five times a week, 52 weeks—that could be another $100 cost). Let someone in the office get married, quit, or have a birthday, and the hat will be passed for contributions for gifts. At Christmas it may be the same, only more.

Any job at all may require a certain amount of wardrobe improvement. Unless your wife sews (if she works, she will hardly have time for that), you can count on an upsurge in the family clothing bill.

Trips to the hairdresser will be more frequent. This is a necessary and unavoidable expense, so count on it.

Meanwhile, back at the ranch, meal times will change, too, when your wife works all day. Either you will use more convenience foods, eat out more often, or cook yourself. The first two cost more than if you or your wife fixed meals from scratch at home.

Every extra procedure needed to process food for sale adds to its cost. Those ready-made, heat-your-own frozen dinners don't come freshly picked from the garden. There are a lot of people in between the farmer and you. Yet often, when both of you work, the convenience of these meals will out-weigh the expense.

If your wife comes home too tired to fix dinner, and if you haven't done it, it may mean a night out at your favorite restaurant. One meal out could pay for half a week's groceries. Dining out like that simply costs much more than eating the same at home.

Most wives want a clean house; most husbands want clean clothes. A working wife may not be able to do justice to both (not to mention meals, sewing, and so forth), unless you pitch in. Even with your help, a maid may be needed. Of course you can both spend weekends cleaning house, washing windows, and mopping floors, but most families, including those of clergymen, prefer to spend some time together doing what they most enjoy. Cleaning house is not often one of those pleasures. So you may decide to hire a maid when your wife goes to work.

Not everything that happens when your wife goes to work involves money. As a pastor's wife, what happens to her relationship with your congregation?

Certainly your congregation did not hire your wife when they called you. They may have thought they did, but I hope you straightened them out on that rather promptly. They hired you.

Your wife may be willing to put herself into your ministry in such a way that she is an extension of the services you are giving. Some wives do that, getting so involved that it is in fact a husband–wife ministry team. It is the traditional at-titude in older, smaller, rural congregations. If it is, a working wife could create some tensions. The two of you will need to handle the matter gingerly.

There are now such husband–wife teams where both are in fact employed by the congregation, and, in some cases, both may be ordained. Then, of course, your wife is already working full time and getting paid for it, and the two of you are doing your job together. God bless you both.

But, that's not usually the case. A working wife will not be as involved in the life of the congregation as she might be otherwise. She cannot attend the Wednesday morning prayer group, she will miss the Tuesday morning women's group luncheon, and vacation church school will be out of the question for her. Even evening meetings may be a problem because her family will want her sometimes. She may not be able to help fold bandages, clean the church, or host visiting dignitaries.

Think about it. It may not make any difference to your ministry if your wife works, then again it may, simply because the people you serve expect her to serve them, too. If your wife decides to work you will need to help smooth the way, and clear the air to avoid potential conflict over it all.

As you look down the road, your wife is working, her job is steady, the pay keeps coming in, you are making ends meet again (even if you are spending more), the congregation is satisfied.

Suddenly, she's out of a job. Laid off. Pay stops.

You have learned (and liked) to live on two salaries. You spend two salaries, too. With only one of you around now to bring home the bacon, you will really have to squeeze to get by unless you cut back on family spending and lower your standard of living.

Obviously that's precisely what you will have to do, unless your wife decides to seek a job somewhere else. Even if she does, the family finances will suffer a severe blow until she finds one. Looking at it now, down the road, it may all seem rather unlikely, but don't ignore the possibilities. It does happen.

Some sort of emergency savings plan will, of course, tide you over for a while (all the more reason to save regularly). But even that won't last forever.

Looking down the road again, your wife is at work, has been for some time, and has a good, steady job. But, the Lord calls, and he calls you—the call is out of town—to another state, another church, another home. What, then, about her job? If it is good enough do you turn down the call for that reason, or do you pull up stakes, your wife quitting her job, and go off to your new church? Again, don't overlook this

possibility. Try to weigh the alternatives now. Try to anticipate what you would do.

That may never be a problem, but if it is, whether it is a
bad one or not depends upon you. What if your wife earns
more at her job than you do at your church? Will that affect
your ministry? Will it hurt your ego, damage your self-
confidence, upset the good relationship you have had with
your wife? It could happen, especially when pastors are poorly
paid. For your pocketbook there would be rejoicing, but for
your subconscious self-respect there may be bitterness and
weeping and gnashing of teeth. No problem? Good, then
forget it; enjoy your abundance, and make the most of what
your blessed wife is doing for the benefit of the family coffers.

The report mentioned a few pages back does not say a
pastor's wife should not work. It only suggests that there is
far more to look at than gross pay. You and your wife will
make the choice, of course. But a realistic listing of all those
extra costs that are bound to come up must be carefully and
systematically reviewed. If the two of you ignore them you
are only fooling yourselves.

Or if she doesn't . . . Maybe your wife doesn't have an
outside job. Chances are good then that she can find ways
to cut costs (beyond what are listed in chapter 2). However,
the advantages or disadvantages of a working wife cannot be
all measured in dollars and cents.

Your wife may be worth her weight in gold as your family's
best tax-dollar saver. She shops for groceries, chauffeurs the
kids everywhere, probably keeps track of the family checkbook, shops for clothes and supplies. In general, she looks
after all those family details you are too busy to get involved
in. As the family money-spender, then, she can be a real help
in getting the best buy for every dollar and also in making
sure you get every tax break that's coming to you.

For wives. Turn the next few paragraphs over to your wife.
I want to talk to her about a few things. Of course, you can
read on, too, if you want, but the you in the next pages is for
her.

As a pastor's wife you probably realize that the only way

Uncle Sam lets a family take any deduction at all on its income tax return is if the husband and wife have kept good records. The key to justifying any reduction in your taxable income is good records. Both of you must record when, where, why, what, who, and how much, to substantiate any deduction. That means if you do most of the spending for your family, you, as does your husband, need some kind of record-keeping system.

Your checkbook, of course, is the best record. Canceled checks are irrefutable evidence of a payment. Live out of your checkbook as much as you can.

But, for all those little miscellaneous cash payments you make, keep a notebook handy. Carry it around with you. Jot down the essential facts anytime you spend money, especially if you think there's a possible deduction available. Keep all bills, receipts, and stubs as further evidence of your payments. Stash these into a manila envelope, one for each month. You'll have a specific record and proof of expenses for the entire year.

Here are the kinds of items you ought to look for:

Medical and dental expenses. Keep tabs on anything you pay doctors, prescriptions you have filled, health insurance premiums, laboratory tests, and, under certain circumstances, special diet foods and transportation of the handicapped.

Taxes. Generally all taxes, except federal taxes, are deductible. Keep a record, especially of unusual sales taxes or gasoline taxes. While there are special tax tables you can use, if your record shows more than the tables allow, you'll be income tax dollars ahead.

Interest. Just about any interest you pay is deductible. Examine your bills and invoices carefully. If you've paid any interest charge, it's deductible. Particularly scrutinize any installment payments you make on your new car, washing machine, or other new appliance. There are bound to be interest and finance charges included. Don't overlook them. They are deductible.

Contributions. When they pass the offering plate at Sunday school or the women's society meeting, jot down what you put in. These are deductions often overlooked. Don't forget your children's Sunday school offering. Remember that every dollar you can deduct, means a minimal 14 cents less income tax you'll pay.

Home entertainment. If you are like the average clergyman's wife, you probably do a certain amount of entertaining at home—guest preachers in for Sunday dinner, overnight guests, visiting missionaries, and similar hosting. You can deduct the costs involved—food, supplies, special maid service, and so on—provided they have to do with church business. Keep a record. Write it down.

Clerical supplies. All professional expenses are deductible. That includes the cost of special uniforms (your husband's clerical shirts and collars, clerical robes, and the like), their cleaning, and repair. Keep the cleaner's stub. It's proof of a professional expense and deductible.

But, most important, write down any expense that looks like it could be deductible. It's worth money in the bank to you.

Saving tax dollars is not the only way you can cut the family's spending budget. As the family's expert on the price of foods (because you do the buying), you can save dollars in the grocery aisles as well. In fact, with thoughtful planning you can probably cut your food bill by 15—20 percent.

Most family food budgets represent about one-fourth of total income. If your income, including parsonage, is about $10,000, you'll spend about $2,500 on food (depending on the size of your family, of course.) Save 10 percent on that and you're talking about $250; 20 percent could be $500.

Many smart shoppers save food money by planning menus a week in advance, according to the supermarket newspaper ads. Lists are prepared noting all items required for the week. A skillful shopper also keeps things flexible enough to make last-minute changes once she's at the store. Those 10-cent oranges may be old and dried. So she looks at another fruit, or shifts from fresh fruit to dried or frozen fruit.

The fewer trips to the store the better. You may select two or three supermarkets to shop each week, but to cut costs plan only one trip each week. Week in—week out planning is essential if you ever expect grocery shopping to make real savings for your budget.

Yet, that's not the way most people seem to operate. A recent study showed that more than half the shoppers tested used no list, many used only a partial list. It seems that fewer and fewer people are really using lists. Do you?

Obviously, you can save on food costs by knowing which prices and brands give the best bargains. Lowest prices and best known brands, of course, aren't always the best buy. Sizes are also deceiving. The only way you can really compare is by weights and measures. You must read labels to get at that kind of information. It's true, you may need a mental calculator sometimes to make comparisons, but fortunately, many products now show cost per ounce, pound, pint, or quart. Once you've decided on quality, price by weight and measure is still the best guide to bargains.

Food cost—saving—planning doesn't end, though, once you get past the checker and have your supplies stored on your pantry shelves. Planning goes on through every day—menu, meal, and between market trips, too. Are you using what you so carefully shopped for and planned to use? Are you using it all? How many space wasters have you forgotten on the shelf? How many meals were prepared so hurriedly you never took the time to use those three-month-old Jello boxes or that six-month-old cake mix, now stale and dry. Is there lettuce spoiling, radishes shriveling, or leftover chicken going bad because you forgot they were there? Wasted food—no wonder your costs seem outrageous.

Plan your buying at the right price; plan your menus to be tasty yet inexpensive; plan your meals soon enough, and you've got yourself the beginnings of a plan to cut food costs.

To be a bit more specific, it's probably the price of meat that has your food budget out of whack. In the months (even years) ahead, you may as well plan to spend a lot more on meat—regardless of cut.

Of course, it's all a better deal for the poor farmer, and I certainly sympathize with his plight. Better incomes for farmers have been long overdue. Perhaps the average shopper is still getting a bargain in the meat that is bought. But, bargain or not, rising meat prices mean a further squeeze on already pinched pocketbooks of most families. With practically no relief in sight, the alternatives narrow drastically. Perhaps there are places you can still cut costs without cutting food value, flavor, or nutrition. Check out the following possibilities:

—The economy of a particular cut or type of meat, poultry, or fish depends on the amount of cooked lean meat it provides as well as its price per pound. Select the ones that give the most lean meat for the money spent. A relatively high-priced meat with little or no waste may be far more economical than a low-priced cut with lots of bone, gristle and fat. Information and recipes are available in Home and Garden Bulletin 43, "Money-Saving Main Dishes," available free from the U.S. Department of Agriculture (hereafter, USDA) Washington, D.C. 20250.

—Don't overlook the specials. They're opportunities to get cuts that normally are out of your budget's reach.

—Meats come marked: USDA prime, choice, and good. Check the labels. For the money, good grade beef has more lean, and usually costs less per pound than choice. Juice and flavor may be less, but food value is the same.

—Nutritious meals include meat, milk, vegetables and fruits, and bread and cereals every day. Yet, you can cut back on the quantity of meat, poultry, and fish with fill-ins, or more economical foods—potatoes, rice, macaroni products, and breads. You'll still need at least one serving of meat, poultry, or fish every day, say USDA home economists.

Be sure you get all the flavor and food value possible out of every piece of meat. Use leftover meats in casseroles, salads, sandwiches, and as flavoring for cooked vegetables. Meat bones can be cooked in soup; meat drippings go in gravies and sauces.

—You can use meat alternates, such as eggs, dried beans, dried peas, and peanut butter. Such foods give protein and nutrients that meats supply. The same amount of proteins is available in one serving of hamburger as in two eggs, one cup of pork and beans, one cup of dry beans, two ounces of peanut butter, or two slices of cheese.

Of course, meats are not the only food prices going up. Other foods have risen just as drastically, and in all likelihood will continue to do so. All the more reason that you may want to read "Your Money's Worth in Foods." It's a USDA booklet available from the Superintendent of Documents, U.S. Government Printing Office, Washington, D.C., 20402. Send 25 cents.

Tune your husband back into this chapter. The rest is intended for him, although, of course, you may wish to read it, too. In fact you may find this whole book more helpful in keeping your husband's pocketbook safely filled, than he. But now back to your pastor-husband.

For husbands. If your wife works, or if she doesn't, the alternatives abound with possibilities. It's a difficult decision to make, fraught with implications, no matter which way the coin falls (but, please, don't make your decision that way).

Only you and your wife together can determine whether she should work. Maybe she should. At least that will be $50 or more a week than you would have had otherwise. Perhaps your wife needs to work to get out of a rut, to feel more useful, or to use special skills that she has acquired. A job can be stimulating and satisfying.

But before you do anything, you'll want to discuss the pros and cons thoroughly, especially if there's a dwindling budget that's got you considering that second paycheck. Think long and hard before you take the plunge.

Of course, your congregation ought to pay you a living wage anyway. Press them for a decent rate, then your wife may not have to work—unless that's what she really wants to do . . . Should your wife work? Well, that all depends.

When You Buy That New Home
4

Whether or not you buy your own home or live in a church-owned parsonage depends on a lot of factors. The pros and cons often balance each other in the long run. And yet (here I show my prejudice), a clergyman will often be ahead financially, eventually, if he has the opportunity to purchase his own home.

This chapter is a discussion of what's involved in purchasing your own home—the tax consequences to be considered with an allowance, and the arrangements you will make for moving into that new place.

From an income tax point of view, having an allowance and owning your home is by far the best deal. You simply pay less income tax that way than if you are in a parsonage or manse. This is true not only because the entire allowance is excluded from taxable income since you use it to provide a home, but because you can also deduct interest and taxes again as you itemize deductions. All of this cuts down your tax significantly.

Later in this chapter we will discuss some of the details you will want to consider as you set up your allowance.

But, first, there are many other considerations than just the tax issue that need to be discussed when you are trying to decide whether to buy a new home. If inflation keeps on the way it has, within the next five years your $30,000 home will be worth $40,000. Buying a home is a good hedge against inflation. Incidentally, retirement planning anticipates a house that is paid for. Owning a home all along in your ministry gives you that chance. A parsonage does not.

Homeownership, among other things, provides (requires) participation in the local taxing program of your community, making your family a very definite supporting part of the community. It will help you to understand your neighbors' homeowning problems better, and in that way, you will be a substantial contributor to the welfare of the community in which you live. You can speak out with more authority perhaps, on those matters where your tax dollars will be used. It's a very personal issue for you, then, because your pocketbook is at stake to support local schools, police, libraries, and other community services.

Another reason for homeownership may be that it provides a keen sense of accomplishment, permanency, attachment, and security. It is to the credit of American clergymen, and their families, that they have usually been quite secure and at home wherever they are, and under whatever circumstances they may be living. Yet, homeownership, unlike parsonage living, provides a sense of freedom. "This belongs to me, and I need not consult a parsonage committee at every turn!" Along with this sense of freedom, of course, goes responsibility. The homeowner cannot call some church committee to look after leaky plumbing in the middle of the night. He has to fix it himself.

A familiar argument for homeownership by clergymen is the idea of building up an equity. Substantial savings or equity can be built up over a period of time, and can amount to a significant sum. On the basis of today's longest term-lowest payment policy, however, it takes quite a while to build up an equity, except through larger down payments. But, few homeowners expect to pay for their homes in full, ever, for they will someday probably move to a larger one. Yet, over a period of time, and coupled with increases in property values, equity actually can be built up which will eventually accrue to the minister's benefit.

Homeownership may very well be an inducement to a longer tenure in one place. It's rather simple to pack up and move out of the church's parsonage, but selling your home and taking care of the details involved may prove to be a real burden. On the other hand, precisely because of the permanency involved in home buying, if the relationship between pastor and people deteriorates after a time, a church may not be able to encourage a pastor to move on as graciously as otherwise. So it works both ways.

Surely the pastor who knows about mortgages, insurance, taxes, escrow accounts, closing costs, interest, and the general problems of house maintenance will be far more familiar with some of the most prevalent and basic problems affecting families today. Obviously homeownership will provide some valuable experience in this area of counseling. Few parsonage clergymen can sit down with their parishioners and, when the situation demands it, intelligently discuss such financial matters with them. They are simply lacking in the necessary experience. There may be a significant effect upon the membership when they know that their pastor is familiar with some of their homeownership problems.

We must also recognize, however, that there are several distinct advantages to living in a parsonage. In those denominations where pastors move or are moved frequently, homeownership would produce considerable hardship and inconvenience. Selecting, buying, and selling a home are not things one would do every three or four years. Doing these things at all takes considerable time. Usually it means an extra move for the new pastor and his family from the rented place they first moved into, to the home they finally select.

Furthermore, not every congregation is located in the kind of neighborhood where a pastor may want to buy a home, or where such an investment is good, or even possible. It is very important for the church to serve the downtown communities of our large cities, but it is not always possible to buy adequate living quarters for a pastor's family in such areas. Congregations in the midst of modern apartment complexes pose similar disadvantages to the purchase of a home.

Sometimes, perhaps quite often, a home is sold for a loss, or at least for less than was initially paid for it. A clergyman must accept this possibility if he owns his home. When figures are finally totaled, the facts may reveal that no more was lost than would have been spent had the man been paying rent. In the meantime, though, there has certainly been the satisfaction of enjoying one's own home and doing with it what one likes.

If your church does offer you an allowance, and you decide you want to buy your new home in that community, you will do well to proceed with caution in taking the next steps. Though it is done frequently, it is not a simple matter to buy a house.

First, you will want to consider cost and size of the new home you have in mind. A good rule of thumb is that the cost of your home should not exceed two and one half times your annual income or, to put it another way, your monthly mortgage payments should not exceed one fourth of your monthly take-home pay. This will set the maximum on the amount you should consider in purchasing a home.

Then, consider the space requirements for your family's needs today, for years to come, and the space you think you would like to have. Then, if you expect to build your home or buy a relatively new one, you can add up the possible costs. A quick estimate, variable of course, depending upon what you include in your home, can be totaled if you know the average cost per square foot for building in your community. Ask a reputable builder for an estimate. Perhaps it will be fifteen to twenty dollars per square foot. If so, compute the total square footage of living space you will need, multiply by the estimated cost, and you have a rough idea of what your house may cost. If the figure is beyond your purchase ability but you need the space, consider buying an older house, one that is roomy and in good condition. Look around your town, and you may find a bargain. Don't forget, though, that it may cost a significant amount to repair and that annual maintenance costs may be large too. While a new home is virtually maintenance free for many years, it does cost more for its size to begin with than an older home will.

So, whether you buy a new home, build on your own lot, or get an old home will depend largely on your tastes, needs, and the costs involved. You will do well to consider carefully all aspects of each situation. Know what you face before you jump off the deep end. Be prepared to face the costs—expect the unexpected—of whatever decisions you make. Houses don't usually come very inexpensively, though you can still find a bargain by careful and patient shopping. No house or lot will be perfect. Make your decisions, then enjoy the freedom of being one of the millions of Americans owning their own homes.

There are yet a few other items which you need to consider rather carefully before you launch out on one of the most expensive projects you will probably ever encounter. You will want to investigate the location of your new home —its neighborhood, shopping centers, schools, buses, and so forth. How close is it to your church and to other churches of the same denomination? Consider the approximate value of the other homes in the area. Don't buy or build a house that is obviously more expensive than the others nearby. Should you want to sell sometime, the proximity to lower-priced houses will tend to reduce the value of your house. A less expensive house in a more expensive neighborhood is better for resale possibilities.

Few young families today expect to live in the house they are buying now for the rest of their lives. As the children grow up, or companies transfer employees, or for any number of reasons—changing neighborhoods, encroachment of industry, freeway construction, etc.—families will sell their homes, move elsewhere, and buy again. Each move will probably be to a higher-priced house, and the cycle of home buying will start all over again. Good or bad, this is the trend in modern America. Clergymen, rather than being an exception to the trend, will probably move even more frequently than most people because of the nature of their occupation. Carefully consider costs, sizes, neighborhoods, conveniences, schools, proximity to business districts, busy streets, and so forth. Don't rush in. Chances are, there's another house for the same price not too far away. Barter for a fair price on what you want. Then get what you want at a price you can afford to pay.

Once you have decided on a particular lot and house, have your banker appraise the property for you. If you are agreed on a purchase price with the seller, you will want to sew up the deal as soon as possible with a formal contract of sale. That is, you can assure the seller that you want the place by signing a contract to that effect, and making a small down payment toward the purchase price. This will bind the seller to sell to you and you to buy at the stipulated price. Otherwise, you forfeit your earnest money payment. You will probably agree in writing to close the deal within thirty days; it usually takes about that much time to get all the necessary papers in order. If you are arranging for a loan, there is a considerable amount of work necessary to complete such arrangements. At any rate, a contract of sale is essential for the protection of both parties, and gives your attorney opportunity to prepare the necessary documents unhurriedly.

Your attorney will be able to prepare all the papers you will need, and he will carefully check over the papers prepared for you by the seller's attorney. Your initial contract should include: full names of both parties, terms of the sale and purchase, legal description of the property involved, any special arrangements regarding furnishings, draperies, carpets, and so forth, guarantee of good title or furnishing of a title policy, return of down payment if financing is not available or for any other stipulated reason, agreement on payment of closing costs and anything else you think necessary for your protection until you get a deed and title to the land.

You will want to arrange financing. Perhaps your congregation will help, at least with the down payment. But the major portion of the money you will need for buying will come from a mortgage loan—either GI, FHA, or conventional. Veterans can take advantage of the lower interest rates on the GI loan. Many homeowners use FHA-backed loans, but the majority of loans are conventional types. In these, you and a banker agree on the amount of the loan, interest rate, and the terms, with no government guarantees to either of you. Interest rates will tend to be higher, of course.

Don't overlook the following items either when you are out shopping for that dream home. Escrow accounts are often established by lending institutions to provide funds for the payment of insurance and taxes for you. If such an arrangement is worked out, your monthly payment will include interest and principal on your loan, as well as one-twelfth of the estimated insurance costs and taxes for the year. Escrow accounts are computed in such a way that whenever your insurance and taxes come due, usually once a year, there will be enough money accumulated in this fund to pay these costs. In a sense your escrow account is a savings plan whereby you make monthly deposits to cover those costs that are due and payable annually.

Fire and extended insurance coverage on your home will be required by the lender in an amount at least equal to your loan. For your own protection, you ought to consider having additional coverage. About 80 percent of the value of your home (not including the land) is sufficient, depending again on the kind of house you have. A reputable insurance agent can give you good advice.

Young families with large mortgages will do well to purchase a life insurance policy with decreasing term. Depending on the amount of the mortgage and your age, it may cost you $5 to $8 a month. It is term insurance, which means there are no dividends, cash, or loan value involved. It is decreasing insurance because the face amount of the policy decreases as the balance owed on your mortgage decreases. Its purpose is to protect the family by paying off the balance of your mortgage in the event of your death.

When you buy property you will also want to protect yourself against claims on the property due to a faulty title.

Your attorney will make an examination of the deed records for you—a kind of history of the property over the past fifty years or so to be certain there are no claims for ownership against it, and that you are actually buying the entire interest in the property. He will also examine the necessary records to be certain that there are no liens or judgments against the property, and that the taxes are paid. He may give you an abstract, a rather bulky book listing all the previous owners, and other information about the property. Or, you may simply receive a letter from him stating that he has examined the deed records and other documents at the county courthouse, and finds no fault with the deed, and no outstanding judgments or liens against the property. In some states you may get a title insurance policy. For a lump-sum premium based on the current valuation of the property or amount of your mortgage, a title company will insure you against defects or claims by others to the title for your lot. In return for the premium paid, the title company guarantees to pay to the mortgage holder or the purchaser (if an additional premium is paid) the face amount of the policy, should anyone ever make an enforceable claim of prior interest in the property against you.

Closing costs are a part of every real estate transaction, and they can be quite expensive depending on the circumstances of the sale. If you are buying an unimproved lot and can pay cash for it, the attorney's fees and recording fees are about all that are involved. On the other hand, if you are purchasing a home, you may get involved with refinancing loan costs, setting up initial escrow account balances, apportioning taxes due, paying attorney's fees, using a title company (and paying for their services), getting title insurance, and a whole host of other items which may involve considerable costs. Be sure of what you have to pay ahead of time. Indeed, secure an itemized list. A few inquiries will get you all the information you need. You will be much better prepared for the closing experience than if you are caught off guard. Unless you and the other party agree differently, seller and buyer share in these costs and pay their respective portions.

If you are in doubt about the boundaries of your property, a survey should be made. A qualified surveyor will prepare a scale drawing of your lot showing boundaries, dimensions, and the locations of all improvements. Furthermore, the surveyor will bury steel rods at each corner of your lot so that you can always locate the corners if you need to.

An independent appraisal is very desirable whenever you are considering selling or buying real estate. It is simply a good idea to have impersonal expert advice about the current worth of the property you are considering. Appraisers are familiar with the market, surrounding land values, the area, the future potential, and many other items you don't know anything about. It may cost you some money, but you will know if the lot and house are worth the price you are bidding or asking.

If you are requesting a mortgage to purchase property, the lending institution will make its own appraisal for determining the maximum amount of your loan—usually about 70 to 75 percent of the total value on conventional loans, but much higher on insured loans. Tax officials will have previously appraised the lot and house for tax purposes, and you can get this information from the proper books of record at the courthouse. This may not be as reliable a value estimate as an independent appraiser's current estimate of worth. Know what you are buying and get a good deal.

The computation of real estate taxes varies considerably from one community to another. The amount of taxes varies, too, depending upon the community and the location of the property. The greater percentage of your property taxes will be for public school purposes, no matter where the property is located. In addition, certain city taxes are received to finance activities for the good of all the people—fire and police protection, street improvements, new sewers, water lines, libraries, and other public services. Real estate taxes become first liens against property if they are not paid, and after a time property can be sold to collect these taxes.

Property taxes are computed on the basis of dollars per hundred or thousand dollars of valuation. If the property is usually appraised at half its real value with the tax rate at $33 per $1,000 valuation, then a $30,000 home would have an annual tax due of $495. Such taxes are usually paid annually for the previous year. Although many agencies may benefit from such taxes, they are usually all paid in one place, at one time, in one lump sum by the property owner. All the taxes collected are divided according to an agreed ratio to the various agencies supported in this manner.

From time to time, cities will make assessments against property owners for paving a street abutting lots on that street. Sewage and water assessments are common when new facilities are constructed. In a sense, these become taxes due and again, are first liens against the property if not paid.

Don't forget to take into consideration the cost of improvements and repairs to your house when you are budgeting for its payment. You won't have a landlord to take care of these items for you. The house will be yours and you will have to pay for its upkeep. Be especially realistic in your family budget, and when you become a home owner, expect the unexpected! *

Your Housing Allowance

Now that you've bought that new home and considered all those home-buying questions, it's important to realize that you must do things correctly with your housing allowance to satisfy IRS requirements. It's the only way you will get full tax benefits. Within all applicable tax regulations, you want to take whatever advantage you can of every tax break you are entitled to, and enjoy every pay advantage you can manage.

With a housing allowance you may be able to avoid a considerable amount of taxes—let me remind you again that that's not evading taxes. You can put money in the

* Adapted from *Money Management for Ministers* by the author and used with permission. Augsburg Publishing House, Minneapolis. 1966.

bank when you avoid paying taxes you don't owe. Do it right, and your housing allowance gives you a good chance to increase your take-home pay and cut your tax.

Here then is how you go about using that housing allowance to the greatest financial advantage for yourself and your congregation.

To begin with, your allowance must be set up according to procedures established by the IRS. For instance, it must be used for certain purposes only, with accounting records made of those uses. Reporting for income tax purposes must be done correctly, and all claims for deductions and exclusions properly substantiated.

The IRS is very explicit about who is entitled to receive and exclude from taxable income a rental allowance. In order to qualify for the exclusion, the house or rental allowance must be provided as remuneration for services which are ordinarily the duties of a minister of the gospel. Examples of such services include the performance of sacerdotal functions, the conduct of religious worship, the administration and maintenance of religious organizations and their integral agencies, and the performance of teaching and administrative duties at theological seminaries.

Specifically, this means that to qualify for the exclusion, you must be an officially ordained minister of your denomination. But, ordination alone is not sufficient. In order to qualify for the exclusion, your housing allowance must also be provided as remuneration for services which are ordinarily those of a minister of the gospel. Essentially, that means that whatever work you do must be normal in the exercise of your ministry.

If you are a commissioned missionary, you are entitled to a housing-allowance exclusion only if you are ordained. A minister of music, education, or administration may exclude a housing allowance from gross salary only if ordained. An ordained minister who performs services in the control, management, and maintenance of a religious organization, or one of its institutions, is considered by IRS as performing duties of a minister of the gospel, and thus qualifies for the exclusion.

If you are not a parish pastor, but work for one of the church's institutions, your housing allowance may be excluded from your gross income. If you would do the same work for an agency not associated with, or which is not an integral agency of, the church denomination, you cannot exclude the allowance.

To qualify as an integral agency of a church denomination, your employing organization must meet the requirements outlined in Revenue Ruling 72-606, 1972:

1) whether the religious organization incorporated the institution;

2) whether the corporate name of the employing institution indicates a church relationship;

3) whether the religious organization continuously controls, manages, and maintains the institution;

4) whether the trustees or directors of the institution are approved by, or must be approved by, the religious organization or church;

5) whether trustees or directors may be removed by the religious organization or church;

6) whether annual reports of finances and general operations are required to be made to the religious organization or church;

7) whether the religious organization or church contributes to the support of the institution; and

8) whether, in the event of dissolution of the institution, its assets would be turned over to the religious organization or church.

Unless most of these conditions are satisfied, an ordained minister may not exclude from income any rental allowance designated by even a church-related organization. Control by the church denomination is the essential condition for an institution to be an integral agency of the church.

Thus, if you're a professor of religion in a church-related school, you may exclude the allowance; if you teach religion in a state school, you cannot. However, if your church specifically assigns you to an institution not an integral agency of a church, such as a state school, then you can exclude your allowance. But, the key to that exception is that you must be assigned to that responsibility by your church.

Unfortunately, military chaplains are specifically denied this exclusion since they are considered to be commissioned officers and not ministers in the exercise of their ministry.

Once your eligibility has been established, and for parish pastors there is no question, then it is important that your congregation take the proper steps to establish, in advance, the amount of your compensation which will include a rental allowance.

To do that, you must specify in writing to your official board precisely how much you will need to provide a home. You should list all those expenses you expect to incur for providing a home. These would include the down payment on your home, the mortgage payments you make (including interest and principal), or the rent you pay, any legal fees incurred in the purchase of your home, bank fees or points you paid to get a loan, any fees you paid for getting a clear title, all your real estate taxes, personal property taxes on your house, special assessments or levies against your property, fire and home liability insurance premiums.

If you make repairs or add improvements to your home, that cost qualifies. Your utility expenses—heat, water, electricity, telephone, sewage, and garbage collection—are all costs for providing a home. If you buy new furnishings, they are included, as well as the costs of appurtenances such as a new garage, sidewalk, or shrubbery.

Of course, you cannot include the cost of domestic help or food, but that is self-evident.

According to the rules you can use your allowance for the items to provide a home. If your entire allowance is so used, you need not report any of the amount as income; it is excluded. Yet, you may still deduct the cost of interest and real estate taxes if you itemize your deductions. On the other hand, if you fail to use all the allowance, the unused portion is taxable and must be included as additional income on your tax return.

Here, then, is the effect on your income tax. Recall that the law permits you to exclude from taxable income (1) the entire allowance providing you used it all, or (2) the rental value of your parsonage. That means you pay no tax at all on that income. That's a clergyman's unique tax break. Your members must pay tax on the income used to buy their homes. You don't, and for that reason your tax is going to be less than a layman's with the same income. Just compare the differences on the chart following.

This is an exception granted to clergymen only. It's the same tax benefit whether you own your home or live in a parsonage. Your allowance, or the rental value, of the church-owned home is simply not taxable income.

On top of that, if you own your home, you may also deduct the interest you pay on your mortgage loan and the real estate property taxes. That makes it a double deduction in a sense. You do not pay tax on the income used to buy your home, nor on interest and taxes paid out of tax-free income. That's a real tax bargain!

Of course, you cannot also deduct depreciation, even if you do use a room in your home for a study. In the normal situation, a businessman can in fact deduct the costs of maintaining an office at home as part of his professional expenses. But, if you receive a housing allowance, you have already excluded from your income that part used to pay for an office. You cannot take another deduction, at least not in this situation. Interest and taxes paid on your home are the only so-called double deduction items permitted.

One caution. For Social Security tax purposes, remember that the housing allowance or rental value of your parsonage is taxable. You include that allowance in income for Social Security tax purposes, but you exclude it for income tax purposes.

As was pointed out before, it is important that you set up that allowance and use it correctly so you can take full advantage of this unique tax break.

You should know, therefore, that the amount of your allowance cannot be excessive, and it certainly cannot be the entire amount of your salary. In fact, a recent ruling by the IRS specifically limits the allowance to a maximum not to exceed "the fair rental value of the house, including furnishings and appurtenances, such as a garage, plus the cost of utilities." Any greater amount designated as a rental allowance, even if so used, will be ineffectual.

HOMEOWNERSHIP TAX ADVANTAGE TO CLERGYMEN

Assume: gross salary of $10,000, married, two children, $1,500 interest and taxes paid on house, $3,500 for exemptions and other deductions.

	Layman who rents	Layman who buys	Clergyman with parsonage	Clergyman who rents	Clergyman who buys
1. Base salary	$10,000	$10,000	$ 7,000	$ 7,000	$ 7,000
2. House allowance	-0-	-0-	-0-	3,000,	3,000
3. Income	$10,000	$10,000	$ 7,000	$10,000	$10,000
4. House allowance exclusion	-0-	-0-	-0-	3,000	3,000
5. Income subject to income tax	$10,000	$10,000	$ 7,000	$ 7,000	$ 7,000
6. Exemptions & deductions	3,500	3,500	3,500	3,500	3,500
7. Total	$ 6,000	$ 6,500	$ 3,500	$ 3,500	$ 3,500
8. Interest, taxes	-0-	1,500	-0-	-0-	1,500
9. Taxable income	$ 6,500	$ 5,000	$ 3,500	$ 3,500	$ 2,000
10. Income tax	$ 1,255	$ 910	$ 595	$ 595	$ 310

That's a $285 tax saving for the homeowning clergyman. He pays $945 less income tax than a layman who rents.

You'll need to follow through on three documents to be certain your allowance is correctly and officially established.

You need to tell your official board how much you expect to spend to provide a home. At the same time, you'll tell them your estimate of the fair rental value of your home. Your allowance will be the lower of the two. It cannot exceed the rental value, and anything you don't spend is taxable anyway. Use a form similar to the following.*

MINISTER'S ESTIMATE OF EXPENSES

To: Name of Church or Organization
From: Rev. . . . .
Subject: Parsonage allowance for 19 . .

The amounts set forth below are an estimate of the payments I expect to make during 19 . . to provide a home.

ITEM   AMOUNT

1. Rent on leased premises or fair rental value of home owned by minister.
2. Garage rental (if not included above)
3. Utilities (gas, electricity, water, heat, telephone, etc.)
4. Insurance
5. Repairs and maintenance
6. Furnishings
7. Other housing expenses—set forth
                                        Total $ . . . .
Date: . . . .

                                    . . . .
                                    Minister's Signature

Next, your official board must record their action in the official minutes. This action must be taken prior to any payment to you of any amount designated as rental allowance. The action should be repeated each year, confirming in writing precisely the amount of your compensation designated for rental allowance.

Use a form similar to that shown hereafter to record the action of your board in their minutes. The record must show

* All three forms illustrated are excerpted from "Minister's Parsonage Allowance and Social Security" by Conrad Teitell. Copyright 1972 by Conrad Teitell. Used with permission.

the amount of your allowance, and the dates for which it is effective.

INSERT FOR MINUTES OF MEETING

The Chairman informed the meeting that under the tax law an ordained minister is (1) not subject to federal income tax with respect to the parsonage allowance paid to him "as part of his compensation to the extent used by him to rent or provide a home" and (2) not subject to federal income tax on the rental value of a home supplied to him rent-free.

> The Board on the . . day of . . . ., 19 . ., after considering the statement of Rev. . . . .
> setting forth the amount Rev. . . . .
> estimates he will be required to spend to rent or provide a home for himself and his family during the year 19 . ., on motion duly made and seconded, adopted the following resolution [or—The Board on the . . day of . . . . 19 . . after discussing the amount to be paid to Rev. . . . .
> . . . . as a parsonage allowance, on motion duly made and seconded, adopted the following resolution]: Resolved that Rev. . . . . receive compensation of $ . . . . for the year 19 . . and a parsonage allowance of $ . . . . for the year 19 . . . [If the minister is to have the rent-free use of a home also state: Rev. . . . .
> . . . . shall also have the rent-free use of the home located at . . . .
> for the year 19 . . and for every year thereafter as long as he is minister of the church.] The parsonage allowance [and rent-free use of a home] shall be so designated in the official church records.

Third, the board's secretary or chairman should send you an official written communication stating their action, and specifying the amount of your rental allowance. Of course, that amount will then appear as a separate line item in your congregation's budget.

WHEN YOU BUY THAT NEW HOME

NOTIFICATION BY EMPLOYER

Date . . . .

Dear . . . .

This is to advise you that at a meeting of the Committee held
on . . . . your parsonage allowance for the
year 19. . was officially designated and fixed in the amount of
$. . . . . Accordingly, $. . . . . of the total payments to you during the year 19. . will constitute parsonage
allowance and the balance will constitute compensation. (You
will also have rent-free use of the home located at . . . .
. . . . for the year 19. .).
Under Section 107 of the Internal Revenue Code an ordained
minister of the gospel is allowed to exclude from gross income
the parsonage allowance paid to him as part of his compensation to the *extent used by him to rent or provide a home*. (He
may also exclude the rent-free use of a home.)

You should keep an accurate record of your expenditures to
rent or provide a home in order to be able to substantiate any
amounts excluded from gross income in filing your federal income tax return.

Sincerely yours,

. . . .

Lastly, once your allowance has been properly established,
it is up to you to keep the record straight on how it is used.
Practically speaking, IRS will never know how you use your
allowance unless they ask and you tell them. The burden is
on you to substantiate whatever amount of your allowance
you used.

You must justify with accurate expense records the entire
use of whatever portion of that allowance you exclude from

income. The Home Purchase and Maintenance Record form can be of help to you.

There's no reporting necessary on your tax return if you use the entire allowance. Yet, you must still keep the record, even though your tax return will show nothing. Any unused allowance, of course, must be reported as other income.

Naturally, you and your congregation must consider many items before deciding if a rental allowance is the best move. We have suggested some of those considerations in this chapter, as well as told you what to do once the allowance has been agreed upon. Follow these procedures and you'll be using your allowance to the best advantage.

HOME PURCHASE AND MAINTENANCE RECORD

Address (or lot location) _____

Deed number _____ Recorded at _____ Vol. ___ Page ___

Lot or house purchased from _____

Builder's name and address _____

Appraised value at time of purchase _____ Date _____

True tax assessed value _____ Annual Taxes _____

Amount of insurance coverage _____ Type of policy _____

Insurance coverage by _____ Phone number _____

Due date of policy _____ Due date of premiums _____

    Price of lot $_____   Down payment $_____

    Cost of house $_____   First mortgage $_____

    Closing costs $_____   Monthly payment $_____

    Other costs $_____   Payment due date $_____

Mortgagee name and address _____

CAPITAL IMPROVEMENTS AND REPAIR RECORD

Date Expense/Capital Imp.	Description	Work by	Cost	Financing

UTILITY EXPENSE RECORD

	Jan	Feb	Mar	Apr	May	Jun	Jul	Aug	Sept	Oct	Nov	Dec
Heat												
Water												
Electric												
Other												

OTHER EXPENSES

	Jan	Feb	Mar	Apr	May	Jun	Jul	Aug	Sept	Oct	Nov	Dec

Moving into Your New Home

Your house has been bought, you have made all the arrangements to take advantage of the tax breaks, and you are ready to call the movers.

Don't get in a hurry though. Even moving your household goods requires some planning and knowledge about what's involved. Know the rules, and your move, cross-country or around the block, can be less hectic.

To begin with, the Interstate Commerce Commission, which has responsibility for making sure movers follow the rules, requires that you be told just about everything you ought to know before and after you get moved. In fact, when you move, your mover will give you a booklet, "Summary of Information for Shippers of Household Goods", that will tell you what to expect and what not to expect from the men who move your furniture.

The actual process of moving can be a traumatic experience for you and your family. If you want to know some of the problems that may be experienced in moving, write to any nation-wide moving agent for copies of their booklets on the subject. It may be helpful to anticipate potential problems, and try to avoid them as best you can.

Moving is never easy, and it is always unsettling, until your family is back into a routine and things have calmed down a bit. It will take a lot of patience and considerable preplanning to take the kinks out of your move. Through it all, though, you will need to stay flexible and allow for alternatives. Plan ahead, keep calm, know what you are doing, and the problems should be minimal.

Here, then, are some of the things you'll want to take care of as you plan your move.

1. Select a reputable mover with care. You can use an agent where you live now, or where you expect to move. In either case the agent will make all the arrangements.

2. Arrange ahead of time for payment. Normally you or your church will have to pay the mover the full cost of moving before your furniture is unloaded from the van. You will have to pay cash or by certified check. However, your church may be able to arrange for credit with the mover and thus avoid that immediate inconvenience at moving time.

3. You may want to pack much of your own goods. It is certainly less expensive that way. Your mover, however, will pack any and everything for you. Be sure, though, that what you pack is done carefully. If the mover packs for you, be sure you both know who will pack what. You may find that special postal rates on books make it less expensive to mail them. However, that way you will have to pack the books yourself. Seventy pounds per box is maximum.

4. Be careful in ordering service. You and the mover must sign an order-for-service form before anything is loaded on the van. That's so you both know precisely what services are to be rendered. Your order will include your name, address, and present telephone number, the address for your new home and for any stops along the way. You will agree on pick-up and delivery dates, how and where your furniture will be weighed. An estimate of the total cost will be given to you

(but you will pay actual costs), and the method of payment will be specified.

5. Arrange for a mutually agreeable pick-up date. You can expect the loading to be done in one day. Any packing will be done a day or so before. A tentative delivery date should also be fixed, but stay flexible. Your mover is not required to deliver on the date agreed, so it may be sometime thereafter. Whenever he does arrive, he will give you three hours to arrive on the scene yourself, unlock the door, and let him start unloading. If you fail to show, or he can't get in touch with you, he'll leave. It will cost you extra to get him back.

6. Pay particular attention to the loading and unloading process. Check off with the mover each item as it goes out the front door. Agree on its condition. When unloading be sure everything is accounted for and that any damages or missing pieces are listed on the inventory sheet. Don't sign the inventory count until you are satisfied that all is in order. You will get payment for damages only if it is noted on the inventory sheet, or you can later prove a loss. Close attention to the inventory count can save hours of grief later on.

7. Your shipment is insured already, but only for 60 cents per pound for each article, and that's not very much. You can get more coverage by paying an additional premium (50 cents per $100 evaluation), if you want full coverage.

Specify what you consider to be the full value. Any claims should be filed with your mover promptly.

A final word of advice is, don't let the moving experience frighten you. It is not easy, to be sure, but millions of families go at it every year. Stay calm, plan ahead, and be flexible. This will help tremendously in making the experience less difficult for everyone concerned.

Social Security for Clergymen*
5

There's nothing new about the fact of Social Security. It has been around for as long as many of us can remember. But there have been many changes since that first 1 percent tax was imposed when social insurance became law in 1936. The original legislation is hard to recognize in the complexities of today's law.

For clergymen there have been changes too. As you know there was a time when a clergyman could not benefit from Social Security, even if he wanted to. This profession, along with several others, simply was not covered. A few years ago, the door was cracked, permitting clergymen who elected to be covered to file an irrevocable request to be covered. Aside from the obvious benefits involved, that choice was a voluntary commitment to pay a tax, a bit unusual to be sure. Nevertheless, that was the only way a clergyman could get involved in this insurance program.

Only recently, however, have clergymen finally come under the provisions of the Social Security laws automatically, as have millions of other people. No longer is the old bug-a-boo of separation of church and state preventing clergymen from

* Portions of this chapter have been adapted from the author's article "Tax Planning for Clergymen" in *Tax Ideas*, copyrighted by Prentice-Hall, 1973. Used here with permission.

taking part. Of course, those who still insist that they cannot participate in Social Security for reasons of conscience—they oppose the church's involvement in social insurance—may file a request for exemption from the tax. If IRS says OK (and purely economic reasons won't let you out), then that clergyman is excused from paying the tax. Obviously he misses out on all the benefits, if he is disabled, dies, or retires.

Social Security legislation contains another quirk, too, unique only to the clergy. In order to avoid any conflicts over church–state separation, Congress elected not to have congregations withhold Social Security tax or pay employes' tax either. So, in spite of the fact that almost every clergyman is employed by some congregation or institution, the laws say he is self-employed, at least for purposes of the FICA tax. For other tax purposes, however, i.e., tax-sheltered annuities, he is an employee.

Furthermore, a clergyman's income is computed differently for Social Security tax purposes than for income tax calculations. His housing allowance is the notable exception there. Certain deductions are handled differently, too, which complicates tax-return preparation for clergymen.

Here are some questions and concerns that face a clergyman as he considers what to do with respect to social security.

(1) Who is covered? Who is exempt?

(2) What is included "in the exercise of his ministry"?

(3) What is included in Social Security income? What is excluded?

(4) How are unreimbursed professional expenses handled?

(5) Can Social Security taxes be withheld from salary?

(6) Is an allowance for Social Security taxes an appropriate item on a congregation's budget?

(7) What rates are applicable to clergymen, and what benefits can a clergyman expect?

1. For many years, while most employee groups were included under Social Security legislation, clergymen were consistently excluded, although most of them were employed by some organization.

Eventually, as professional self-employed persons were

covered, clergymen also had an opportunity to join. Between 1955 and 1968 clergymen were eligible for Social Security, provided they filed a waiver form having their exemption from coverage removed. Once filed, such clergymen were permanently included in Social Security, and paid the self-employment Social Security tax.

For taxable years beginning in 1968, all clergymen were finally covered on a self-employed basis for services performed in the exercise of their ministry. Yet, for those who had religious or conscientious scruples about participation, and who never filed the old Form 2031 (Certificate of Election), exemption was still possible. Form 4361 must be filed with the appropriate statement of opposition to this type of public insurance. The form must be approved by IRS before exemption is possible. It is obviously not a ground for exemption to plead that one cannot afford to pay the tax!

Until April 15, 1970, all clergymen on a calendar year basis (who filed their tax returns as of the end of December each year), had the chance to file exemption, provided they had not previously waived it under the old rules. Since then, however, eligibility for filing exemption has been limited to that time, prior to the end of the second year, for which the clergyman nets $400 or more from self-employment. After those two years, a clergyman is forever covered by Social Security if his exemption was not approved. From then on he pays the tax and, of course, gets all the benefits.

2. Not all clergymen are necessarily covered by these regulations. However, some ordained ministers may be treated as any employee, regardless of their ordination, and not be subject to the self-employment tax at all. It depends upon the source of the clergyman's income. Ordination and the conduct of religious services are not the only criteria for coverage.

To be self-employed, the clergyman must qualify, as for the housing allowance. If in fact the clergyman is employed by an integral agency of the church, then he qualifies for Social Security self-employment, provided he performs services in the exercise of his ministry. Such services include the administration of sacerdotal functions, the conduct of worship, and the control, conduct, and maintenance of religious organizations and their integral agencies, under the authority of a church or church denomination.

Such service normally includes the work of all ministers in congregations, seminary professors and administrators, church-controlled college teachers, administrators and other ordained employees, church agency executives, and the like. Employees of any governmental unit are not considered performing services in the exercise of their ministry, even though as a chaplain the administration of sacerdotal functions or the conduct of religious worship is, in fact, done. Thus, military chaplains are not considered self-employed for Social Security or housing allowance purposes. The same is true of Veterans Administration hospital chaplains, or any chaplain employed by a governmental agency.

3. The calculation of the self-employment Social Security tax includes all income reported for income tax purposes, plus the rental value of a parsonage, or the housing allowance.

4. If a portion of unreimbursed professional expenses was not deducted for income tax purposes because it was attributable to earning the tax-free parsonage or housing allowance, all these expenses can be deducted from total income for Social Security tax purposes.

5. Social Security taxes cannot be withheld for a clergyman by his employer unless a separate agreement is finalized, with the church to withhold and forward such monies to IRS. In any event, a clergyman must still calculate the Social Security tax on his own tax return and pay the tax personally, either by excess income tax withholdings or with quarterly estimated payments.

6. Because clergymen must pay their own Social Security taxes, far-sighted congregations have taken an important step in easing the burden of that tax on the clergyman's pocketbook each year. Congregations have established an allowance for Social Security in their annual budgets equaling the maximum Social Security self-employment tax for that year.

By doing so, the congregation assumes its rightful financial obligations, and provides the pastor with an annual built-in salary advance each year the tax increases.

Here's how: In 1972 the maximum tax was $675, in 1973 it . was $864, and in 1974 will be $1,056. If the clergyman had no allowance for this purpose, he would have made up that difference every year out of his own pocket. Assuming his salary increase for the year at least equaled the increase in tax, dollar-wise he stayed even. But, if he got no increase, he actually had a salary reduction.

On the other hand, with an allowance, and the congregation agreeing to pay the full amount each year, the congregation actually pays the increase. Thus, the pastor's take-home pay has not changed (except by the small additional income tax he must pay on the increased allowance), since the congregation foots the bill. Actually, his total pay has gone up just a little bit more than it would have otherwise because the congregation provides an allowance. In fact, a clergyman may want to consider reducing his salary by the amount of the allowance the first time around (if the congregation is reluctant toward setting up that allowance).

That allowance can be paid to the pastor monthly, quarterly, or when it is most convenient for him and his church. But, whatever the procedure, the allowance is still income subject to income and Social Security tax.

7. Now, as you continue paying that tax, and as it continues going up, you will ask yourself more than once, what will I ever get out of it all? If you're younger, the question is even more of a burning issue because it seems so long until retirement and then what? An older clergyman looks forward to the obvious benefit he will soon enjoy with his monthly check.

For some of us it will be a long time until we actually get anything back, that is if we're only waiting until we're ready to retire. Yet, retirement income is not the only coverage your Social Security tax dollar is buying for you. You're buying immediate disability and death benefit coverage as well. If it's needed, you or your family could receive monthly Social Security benefit checks each month.

Most of us forget that we are buying these additional

coverages through Social Security, at a cost competitive with the commercial market. When your Social Security tax seems overbearing, and you wonder if you'll ever see the day when you can get your money back, remember that you're buying important coverage for the present that will pay you and your family significant benefits if you are disabled and can't work or if you die today. You'll get back far more then, than you

COMPARISON OF NET TAKE-HOME PAY WITH OR WITHOUT A SOCIAL SECURITY ALLOWANCE

Assume in 1971 a reduction in salary just to get an annual Social Security allowance started. In subsequent years no other salary increases are received except increase in Social Security allowance to maximum amount.

	1971 w/o	1971 w/	1972 w/o	1972 w/	1973 w/o	1973 w/	1974 w/o	1974 w/
1. Salary	12,000	11,415	12,000	11,415	12,000	11,415	12,000	11,415
2. Allowance	-0-	585	-0-	675	-0-	864	-0-	1,056
3. Income	12,000	12,000	12,000	12,090	12,000	12,279	12,000	12,471
4. Exemptions & deductions	4,000	4,000	4,000	4,000	4,000	4,000	4,000	4,000
5. Taxable income	8,000	8,000	8,000	8,090	8,000	8,279	8,000	8,471
6. Income tax (estimated)	1,600	1,600	1,600	1,618	1,600	1,650	1,600	1,680
7. Income after tax	6,400	6,400	6,400	6,472	6,400	6,629	6,400	6,791
8. Social Security tax	585	585	675	675	864	864	1,008	1,056
9. Net income	5,815	5,815	5,725	5,797	5,536	5,765	5,392	5,735
10. Exemptions & deductions added back	4,000	4,000	4,000	4,000	4,000	4,000	4,000	4,000
11. Net take-home pay	9,815	9,815	9,725	9,797	9,536	9,765	9,392	9,735
12. Additional take-home pay when allowance provided		-0-		72		229		343

First column in each year is income without an allowance; second column assumes an allowance equal to the maximum Social Security self-employment tax.

ever paid. It's small comfort perhaps, when you plunk down that $1,000 a year for coverage, but it's a benefit to you nevertheless.

Under present legislation, Social Security acts as a hedge against inflation. Beginning in 1975, benefits will automatically be increased with a rise in the cost of living. That means you don't have to plan against any erosion in the purchasing power of your expected benefits. They'll simply keep going up as inflation increases.

To find out how much income you can expect to receive from Social Security when you retire, you'll have to determine your earnings, then ask your local Social Security office to give you an estimate of retirement benefits.

You may already have a record of earnings; but, to make sure that records in the Social Security administration office agree with your own, you can request a statement of earnings. Simply mail postcard Form OAR-7004 (available at your local Social Security administration office or post office) to Baltimore, Maryland 21203. You'll get a print-out of your Social Security records which will help your local office give you an estimate of possible benefits.

As you know, benefits are tied to earnings, not to the tax you pay. Thus, self-employed persons, including clergymen, actually pay more out of their own pockets for the same benefits any retired employee receives. What you earn, not the tax you pay, is the basis on which your benefits are figured.

Depending upon the year you reach sixty-five, the following chart illustrates the monthly benefit under existing legislation, assuming you've paid the maximum tax each year.

Only the basic amount you'll get is shown. Depending upon how fast the cost-of-living index goes up, you'll get more. For example, if prices go up just 2¾ percent a year (roughly the current rate), a sixty-five-year-old couple retiring in 1987 will get $783 a month. At that rate, if you're age thirty-eight now, and you retire at age sixty-five, you may end up with a monthly Social Security retirement check of $1,148!

In the meantime, sad to say, the tax keeps going up with no end in sight. But, as benefits are hiked, the tax must be

SCHEDULE SHOWING CERTAIN SOCIAL
SECURITY BENEFITS

Age now	Year of retirement	Benefit for single retiree at age 65	Benefit for married couple both 65
65	1973	$266.10	$399.20
63	1975	283.20	424.80
58	1980	323.40	485.10
53	1985	342.50	513.80
48	1990	353.30	530.00
43	1995	361.50	542.30
38	2000	378.50	567.80

hiked to pay those commitments. Social Security is unlike commercial insurance pension plans. Your tax no longer funds your benefits. You and I and all other people who are still paying the tax today, are helping to finance the fatter checks retirees are getting each time the benefits are pushed up.

Someday, perhaps, we'll cash in on that deal, too. Unfortunately, even $1,148 by the time we retire may not seem as much as it does now. Whatever the amount, though, for most of us it will be very welcome and will go a long way toward helping us keep our family budget balanced.

Remember that Social Security is not only a tax you pay; it is also an insurance and a pension plan. You are buying valuable protection in case of your disability or death, and accumulating for yourself and your wife a pension payment. Even if you don't have much of a choice and can't count on a level premium (tax), it is still a bargain and a benefit. Consider it so the next time you pay the tax!

Getting Around by Car
6

Handle your automobile allowance correctly and you can raise your take-home pay.

You probably already receive some kind of reimbursement for the professional expenses you incur in using your own automobile on church business. Normally your allowance will be stated in terms of so many dollars a month, so many cents a mile, or if you're fortunate, full reimbursement for all expenses.

In place of an allowance, your congregation may have title in its name to a car, with full use given to you for church business. Or, your congregation may lease or rent an automobile for your exclusive use, bearing the entire expense itself. Whatever the situation, you probably do have some kind of reimbursement arrangement with your congregation, or you should.

A professional expense. This is the way it should be. Yet too often the reimbursement does not cover your full expense. If it doesn't, the portion you pay becomes an added financial burden to your already pinched pocketbook. Many congregations now realize that the pastor's use of an automobile is a professional expense, and full reimbursement of all costs should be made. So, if you still pay part of your business-car expenses, your congregation is actually forcing you to support part of the church's legitimate expenses out of your base salary.

You should make it perfectly clear to your official board at the outset, that when you travel on church business the congregation should foot the entire bill. That's a business expense, a professional expense which, as in any commercial enterprise, is normally paid by the employer. You should insist on the same treatment on the grounds that the church, not you, is responsible for the expense of providing a ministry to the membership. Your gas and oil are part of that expense.

You should also make it clear to your official board that your automobile allowance is not compensation. It is reimbursement for your business-related expenses incurred in operating your car for purposes of carrying out your ministry in your community. It ought to be listed as an administrative expense, not as compensation.

Allowance, lease, church-owned? Try to get your congregation to agree to reimburse you for your full expenses in getting yourself around town on church business. That way they must decide whether to provide you with an allowance equal to your total expense in using your own car, or to buy or lease a car for your use.

A decision may depend on whether you already have your own automobile and would have to sell. There are good reasons why using your own car may be best anyway. Of course, if your church decides to provide an automobile for you, you'll take it, and may have to sell your second car to cut down your personal expenses.

In any event, you ought to compare the costs of leasing or owning a car on a full-time basis. Chances are that a lease may cost more than what you now pay to operate your own car, since car rental companies include a profit in their charges. Compare before you make a commitment.

Even if the church takes title to a car for you, the congregation's expenses could get out of hand unless a firm, decisive policy is set down in advance for repairs, tire replacement, and trade-ins.

Using a leased car or the church's car could limit your free use of the vehicle. You can use your own car for pleasure or business, as you like. Some church elder may not be particularly pleased to see you driving off to the beach in the church-owned car! It can be done in your own car with no questions asked.

There is no way to tell you here which way you really ought to go. You've got to check out the costs in your community both ways. Only be sure you include all costs on both sides, as well as conveniences and inconveniences. Then decide. But whatever you do, if things get out of hand one way, keep the option open to go back to a better way.

Allowance arrangement. Assuming that you, like most clergymen, own your car, make all decisions—repair, replacement, color, size, use, and similar concerns yourself—and that the congregation has agreed to reimburse you for the full cost of providing that car when you use it on church business, what is the best financial arrangement—a stated monthly dollar amount, a cents-per-mile allowance, actual cost reimbursement, or something else?

The typical arrangement is so many dollars paid in equal monthly installments. That's generally the least complicated way, but it is not necessarily the most favorable way. Depending on how much time you want to spend to keep the necessary records to justify a more equitable arrangement, you may want to select a different option.

Second only to receiving reimbursement for all professional expenses, income tax regulations suggest one of the best and least complicated reimbursement procedures. The IRS permits two options. On your tax return you can either list all your actual expenses—including depreciation—and take a deduction for the business-related portion of those costs, or you can do things the easy way—deduct a flat 12 cents per mile up to 15,000 miles and 9 cents a mile thereafter for business use, and forget all about your actual costs.

Here's how that works, as shown on the following schedule.

COMPUTATION OF ALLOWABLE
CAR-EXPENSE DEDUCTION

	1971	1972	1973
Assume—			
Costs: Depreciation *	$ 600	$ 600	$ -0-
Gas, oil, etc.	500	500	500
Repairs, maintenance	200	800	500
Tires, battery, etc.	100	500	150
Total costs	$1,400	$2,400	$1,150
Mileage:			
Total mileage	20,000	18,000	16,000
Mileage for church	16,000	14,400	12,800
Percentage for church use **	80%	80%	80%
Then:			
Allowable actual cost deduction	$1,120	$1,920	$ 920
Allowable mileage deduction:			
First 15,000 miles @ 12 cents	$1,800	$1,728	$1,536
Additional miles @ 9 cents	90	-0-	-0-
Allowable mileage deduction	$1,890	$1,728	$1,536
Deduction reported on tax return	$1,890	$1,920	$1,536

* Depreciation calculation: Date of purchase—Jan. 1, 1969. Cost, $2,600 with
$200 salvage. Depreciation rate 25%. Annual depreciation—$600 ($2,600
less $200 times 25%). Depreciation schedule: $600 each year for 1969
through 1972. No depreciation after 1972.
** IRS accepts a reasonable percentage of miles driven.

As you can tell, it is important to calculate the deduction
both ways before you decide which to use. You can change
back and forth from one year to the next, if you like, provided
you haven't used one of the accelerating depreciation methods.
If you have, you'd have to stick to the actual cost method
thereafter. Most clergymen figure depreciation, whenever they
use it, on a straight line basis as in the example. It's the
easiest way.

Once you have made both calculations, the decision is
relatively simple. You take the deduction that gives you the
largest amount. As in the example, actual costs in 1972 provided the most deduction that year; in 1971 and 1973 the
12 cents–9 cents-per-mile deduction was best.

Request to official board. With that kind of possible choice, and based upon your experience in the past, you approach your official board with your request for a reimbursement arrangement. You toss out the fixed allowance as a possibility from the start. It's not tied to your professional expense reimbursement at all and, if you can swing the change in tradition, should not be the basis for payment of your allowance.

Assuming you want to keep title to your own car, or are willing to buy a second car if necessary, you propose a reimbursement plan for professional expenses equal to whatever your total costs will be for the year, including replacement (depreciation). You'll be paid actual costs, but for budget purposes you'll have to estimate an amount. This could be the best arrangement for you.

If that arrangement doesn't seem viable, you can suggest the cents-per-mile plan. Short of total reimbursement, this may give you the best response. Because of the IRS regulations that permit you to deduct 12 cents a mile for at least the first 15,000 miles, no matter what your allowance arrangement, you may be able to get the most favorable agreement with this suggestion. Simply propose that the congregation reimburse you at the popular rate of 10 cents per mile (minimum) for each mile you drive your car on church business. For budget purposes, you'll have to estimate the annual amount, but your record keeping can be simplified and you will be paid for actual miles driven.

Under the 10 cents-per-mile allowance arrangement, all you need do to collect the allowance is tell your treasurer each month how many church-related miles you drove. You still should keep records of actual expenses so you can determine which deduction is most favorable. But, all IRS cares about, if you take the 12 cents–9 cents-per-mile deduction, is your contemporaneous diary showing time, place, business purpose, and number of business miles traveled. It's simple enough to work out a system for keeping that record. You can design one yourself. Just keep it on the dashboard and write down expenses and miles whenever incurred.

REPORT FORM FOR TIME, PLACE, PURPOSE, AND MILES DRIVEN ON CHURCH-RELATED BUSINESS

Date	From-To	Odometer	Miles
		End	
		Start	
		End	
		Start	
		End	
		Start	
		End	
		Start	
		End	
		Start	
		End	
		Start	

In most instances the 10 cents-per-mile allowance and the corresponding 12 cents-per-mile deduction will be the most favorable arrangement for you. But, whatever arrangement you work out should be based on your own facts and figures. After all, the allowance you request may depend on whether you've got a compact car or a gas hog, a newer car or an older one, two cars or one.

More take-home pay. Based on this example, the chart below shows how the 10 cents-per-mile allowance can raise your take-home pay with some tax-free income.

For your congregation's budget, you'll need to estimate total miles for the year. But you can only receive reimbursement for miles actually driven.

There is, however, no best way to set up your car allowance arrangement. You've got to make your own cost study as well as decide on the kind of arrangement you personally prefer and your congregation prefers. The point is that you can probably get better mileage out of your car allowance than you are now getting if you calculate the relative costs of alternatives.

It doesn't make much sense to have your salary reduced

TAX-FREE INCOME
WITH CENTS-PER-MILE CAR ALLOWANCE

Assuming the same facts as in the previous example for "Computation of Allowable Car Expense Deduction"

Net expense deduction:	1971	1972	1973
Total business miles	16,000	14,400	12,800
Deduction reported on tax return	$ 1,890	$ 1,920	$ 1,536
10 cents per mile reimbursement	1,600	1,440	1,280
Net expense deduction	$ 290	$ 480	$ 256
Tax-free income:			
10 cents per mile reimbursement	$ 1,600	$ 1,440	$ 1,280
Actual costs for church use of automobile	1,120	1,920	920
Net cash received (or paid out)	$ 480	$ (480)	$ 360
Tax-free income	$ 480	$ -0-	$ 360

just because your auto allowance isn't being handled in the best way. And, if you are the only one who can do anything about it, perhaps these few suggestions will generate ideas for better ways of arranging that allowance.*

* Portions of this chapter have been excerpted from an article by the author in *Church Management*, December 1972, and are used here with permission.

Investment Ideas for Clergymen
7

You may not want to read this chapter, or at least you may not see any point in doing so. When you're already spending every dime you make and maybe more, what's the sense of knowing how to invest? If you've nothing to save, why bother with the basics of investment strategy and financial analyses anyway?

Why bother with investments when your salary is already so low you can't afford to take your wife out to dinner? When your pocketbook is pinched, there seems to be no end to the need to stretch your dollars. Leaving them lie, untouched, in some bank account makes no sense at all—or so the arguments go.

The truth of the matter is, you really cannot afford *not* to invest (to save). Believe it or not, you'll probably be investing anyway, whether you want to or not, as you spend for some things.

For example, your church's pension plan saves money for you, for your own good; so does Social Security. They're both part of a long-range plan to force you to put something aside for financial support for retirement. If you do not live to retirement, the funds help your widow. You really should invest if you are at all concerned about your family's welfare.

The present cannot be ignored, of course, for it too requires a personal plan for setting something aside for a rainy day. From time to time you may need to draw on savings for an emergency. Investments offer additional income for now and later. And, while we may think retirement income is our only goal for investing, the need for immediate resources may be a far more crucial need sometimes. In either case, an investment plan is required.

Whether you read through this chapter or just skip over it, I hope you won't overlook the need for a specific savings plan (investments) for today. If you can't afford to save, or think you can't, you really should anyway, somehow. Doing so offers you the chance of making sure you'll have what you need when you need it, financially.

There's a rule of thumb which suggests that the only money you should invest in anything (especially stocks and bonds) is money you can afford to lose. Certain savings accounts are in fact insured, at least up to some maximum limits, by an agency of the federal government, so that you can't lose them. But investments in stocks, bonds, mortgages, or real estate are not insured or guaranteed by anyone, let alone the federal government. You'll do best to take the prudent path. Don't invest any money at all unless you can afford to lose the whole bundle.

A second rule is like unto the first. Put together an emergency savings plan before you call your broker on a hot tip.

That doesn't mean that you should be so cautious that you don't invest in anything. You'll do well to put your money where it will grow, not shrivel up. Common stocks offer that opportunity, savings accounts don't. The reverse is true, too. When the bottom drops out of the market, you may never get your money back. Your savings account will still be there. It's an uncertain path for the investor, but over the years with prudent investing, your money can grow —in a savings account it won't.

In this discussion, reference to investments will usually not mean the typical savings account in a bank or savings and loan association. Even that savings account is an investment, strictly speaking; but our reference to investments will normally mean securities and properties that are not savings accounts.

A clergyman may have every intention of making wise and prudent investments; he may even have the resources to do so. But our initial caution remains. Whenever you begin to invest, you do so at your own risk, and only when your emergency savings plan is tucked safely away in your hip pocket (at your nearest savings and loan). When a financial crisis hits your pocketbook, that savings account could be your blessing. Your investments may have all flittered away (not likely, but certainly possible).

So, what is a clergyman supposed to do? May I offer a clue or two?

Before you invest. Make sure you're involved in a regular savings plan. That means no matter how small your salary, how meager your take-home pay, or how pinched your pocketbook, you're putting something away every month. It means you're putting it in a safe place, too, like that bank or savings and loan association just mentioned.

Maybe it's only $5 a month. Hopefully it's much more. But even at $20 a month and earning 5 percent, you can accumulate $1,365 in five years. Do nothing and you'll never see that kind of money anywhere. Save regularly and you'll probably make ends meet, at least. In five years you'll have more than a thousand dollars safely stashed away.

HOW YOUR SAVINGS CAN GROW

How Savings Grow	$5 monthly	$10 monthly	$15 monthly	$20 monthly	$25 monthly	$50 monthly	$100 monthly
6 months	$ 30.45	$ 60.88	$ 91.33	$ 121.76	$ 153.21	$ 304.39	$ 608.78
1 year	61.66	123.29	184.95	246.58	308.24	616.44	1,232.88
2 years	126.47	252.86	379.33	505.71	632.18	1,264.28	2,528.56
3 years	194.58	389.03	583.60	778.05	972.63	1,945.13	3,890.26
4 years	266.15	532.13	798.29	1,064.27	1,330.42	2,660.66	5,321.33
5 years	341.38	682.53	1,023.91	1,365.06	1,706.44	3,412.65	6,825.30
10 years	779.04	1,557.56	2,336.60	3,115.12	3,894.16	7,787.80	15,575.59

This schedule is based on a rate of 5% a year with earnings added and compounded quarterly.

Financial experts make many decisions simply by using some rule of thumb. In addition to the rule we mentioned earlier, there's another one which suggests a possible goal for your savings plan. Since the wise investor doesn't put all of his money into savings accounts, eventually he accumulates sufficient savings and can venture down other paths. The rule of thumb suggests that a savings plan should accumulate about four to six months salary equivalent before beginning on another tack.

The purpose of that is to provide the funds you'll need, temporarily, when you're disabled, out of work, or need quick money for some emergency. Depending upon your insurance program, you may have those eventualities fairly well covered. Of course your congregation would probably look after you for a while if you needed help. Nevertheless, an accumulation of several thousand dollars should be your goal.

Of course, at $20 a month it's going to take a while to amass that fortune. But once you've started, you've won half the battle. The fund will grow, and someday you'll be pleased you took the first step way back when. You just don't dare wait until you think you can afford to save to begin. You can't afford not to save.

Make sure your savings plan is going along well before you invest in something else. Then, before you buy that first share, make certain that your health, disability, and life insurance programs are all well under way. You can plan a program with a qualified insurance agent (a C.L.U. is best). Chances are your own denominational pension-board executive can offer pointers, too.

But before you dive into the Dow Jones, be certain your life insurance is adequate (six times your annual pay), that you have some kind of disability coverage for that long-term illness (to supplement Social Security), and that your health insurance (including a major medical feature) will cover the major costs of hospital and surgical expenses for you and your family.

Only then, when you have that emergency savings fund

well in hand and your insurance plan in good shape, can you afford to take a flier into the world of stocks and bonds. When you can finally afford to lose what you invest (not that you want to, of course), then it's time to shop around for bargains in the market's cellars.

How to buy stocks. There are more than 30 million people who own shares of stocks in the United States. Many of those shares were purchased decades ago, some just today. In fact, millions of shares are bought and sold every business day of the year at stock exchanges across the nation. It's a bigger business than ever, and many people are involved, even clergymen.

If you've never bought stock because you didn't know how to go about it, forget your reluctance and plunge ahead. Assuming you follow the advice in previous paragraphs, a simple phone call is all it takes to buy or sell.

Knowing how to buy stocks is really only a minor consideration. The decision to buy or sell dare not be contingent upon the ease of making a transaction. That convenience has encouraged a lot of people to get on the band wagon. Nevertheless, investment decisions are made to gain income or add value (growth). There's a whole host of considerations that go into buying and selling stocks, and the serious investor explores all he can.

Now obviously no one can guarantee that any investment in stocks will grow in value, or yield any income. That's one of the problems with that kind of investment. Put your money in the bank, and you're reasonably sure of getting it all back, if you want. Not so with stocks. Deposits in most bank accounts are insured by the federal government's agencies, but no one insures the value of stocks.

In a bank, you'll get back whatever you put in, plus interest. With stocks you could get more, you could get less, and dividend income can never be guaranteed. Bank accounts don't grow in value at all, stocks may.

At a bank (or savings and loan association), you'll get a fixed return on your investment. But because the yield may be so low, the interest may not even cover the loss in value of your principal investment. As the years go on, the relative value of that investment may, because of inflation, actually decrease. But with stocks, the value may go up or down; you could come out far ahead or dead broke.

Once decided, here's what you do. Find yourself a good, well-known stockbroker. He's the man who takes your order, and through his membership with one of the national stock exchanges, finds a customer for the stock you've decided to sell, or an owner in case you're ready to buy. That's the beauty of the system of stock market exchanges. They are a central marketplace where buyers and sellers can go to sell or buy their stocks. You don't have to go around looking for someone who may be interested in your particular shares, nor do you have to find someone who has the shares you want to buy. Through your broker and his firm, the market floor is the place for buyers and sellers to get together.

Thus, a broker is your key to getting the stocks you want. How do you find one? Well, every large town has one or more offices of some firm. Check the yellow pages. Look under stockbrokers. Several may be listed, maybe none. An office in your own town is the best to work with if you can. That way you'll get to know the broker personally. Furthermore, it's less difficult that way to sell the stocks you own, although it's easy enough to do so by mail.

A local broker will be more interested in the business you give him, and he'll be more eager to help you than someone outside or unknown to you. Many of the financial resource materials that you'll find most helpful in your search for good investments will be in his office.

It's a good idea to ask around among your friends or members of your congregation for suggestions. Perhaps they will recommend the firms they do business with or one they know. At any rate, you've got to find a broker and open up an account with him if you expect to buy and sell stocks.

Normally you'll have a regular account with your broker whereby you promise to pay within five business days any amount due on securities you purchase. The broker in turn will pay you, also within five days, the proceeds of any sales you request.

More sophisticated shareholders may open margin accounts. That permits them to borrow from their brokers up to 35 percent (the current rate, although that changes from time to time) of the purchase price of certain securities. Of course, those investors then pay interest on that loan, say 8 percent, and someday they'll have to pay it off, either by selling shares held by the broker for them, or remitting cash direct. If you're a beginner, without many dollars to invest, you probably should avoid a margin account.

Buying stocks should not be a willy-nilly procedure. Nor should you put in an order every time you get a hot tip. A careful analysis of securities that fit into your investment plan—income, growth, speculation, or whatever—must be made. Usually, however, clergymen have neither the time nor the experience (nor the expertise) to make such a careful, detailed study. You must depend on others.

For small investments, you can depend upon the advice of your broker. You can make a reasonably safe investment in the shares of almost any of the large familiar companies you know by name. But listen to your broker. His advice can be helpful.

Needless to say, advice from the same person who earns a commission when you act on his suggestion, can color your broker's recommendations. That's why it is important to pick someone you can trust, someone offering advice you can use, not just interested in making money for himself.

For larger amounts, say more than $25,000, wise investors seek the services of professional investment counselors. Such persons are not brokers and do not sell or buy stocks for you. For an annual fee these professionals will suggest to you the investments you ought to make. Reputable investment counsel is important when your portfolio amounts to thousands of dollars.

Once you've picked your broker, opened an account with him, mustered the cash you'll need to buy the stock you've picked, you simply tell your broker to buy so many shares of

XYZ corporation. You can give him a verbal order in his
office, you can write him a letter, or you can telephone him.
He'll accept your request, place your order, and usually within minutes (if you've placed your order at current market
price), tell you the deal is done and give you costs or sale
price. It's that simple whether you buy or sell.

As you can tell, being a shareholder in American business
is really a simple process. But more important than the
procedure, of course, are your investment plan and the stocks
you pick. If you know what you want to do, your broker can
follow through on the mechanics. And, a few weeks after
you've bought, you'll receive your certificate of shares. Then,
you'll be one of those 30 million shareholders, and a part
owner of some vital link in your nation's economy.

An investment plan. "Have a plan and stick to it." That's
the consistent sage advice of David L. Babson and Company,
Inc., Investment Counsel. It was true decades ago and it's
still true today, claims Mr. Babson. But, he states, "We
doubt that the typical investor of our era has been approaching his task as soundly or as effectively as his counterpart of
earlier periods. For in recent times there has been far more
emphasis on following the day-to-day movements of share
prices than on attempting to analyze and understand the
businesses of the companies themselves."

Continuing in their weekly staff letter the Babson organization goes on to say:

> We would guess that the nation's "old" share-
> holders—and nearly all of the 10 million newcomers of
> the past five years—believe that the high road to in-
> vestment success is through "buying low and selling
> high" and repeating the process over and over. To
> their "sophisticated" way of thinking, a stock is
> nothing but a piece of paper on which to make an
> easy profit as it "goes up."
> Yet with what has happened in the securities
> markets in 1969–1970, it ought to have become ob-
> vious to all that the buy-low, sell-high philosophy is
> a cruel myth. When attempted repeatedly, it is bound
> to produce poor—even disastrous—results, because it

requires a fortuitous combination of shrewdness, courage, independence, timing and luck that no human will experience consistently.

A further drawback of this approach is that it causes investors—whether individuals or institutions—to be preoccupied with the daily stock numbers and it prevents them from doing the one thing that is certain to lead to good results—establishing a sound long-range program suited to their financial needs and objectives.

Almost any plan is better than no plan at all. Yet far too few investors ever bother to set up one and, of those who do, far too many do not stay with it through thick and thin. In periods of heady optimism, such as 1967–68, they are lured by tips, rumors, greed and bad advice into speculating when they should be investing. Then in pessimistic years like 1970, they become discouraged.

So after every bear market, millions of what started out to be investment portfolios end up with an illogical assortment of cats and dogs selling at a fraction of what they cost. Then the big question becomes whether to sell out the junk at sickening losses in order to buy good stocks or to wait and pray for a speculative rebound.

Yet this whole can of worms can be avoided if the investor first asks himself some basic questions. How can he construct a sensible plan? What considerations should guide him in selecting suitable holdings? What attitude must he take when market psychology swings from optimism to pessimism, or vice versa?

The first point every investor ought to realize is that his own objective may differ markedly from that of the widow next door, his doctor, golf partner, or alma mater. A 45-year-old business executive whose highly taxed earnings comfortably exceed his living expenses obviously does not have the same investment requirements as a charitable endowment which pays no taxes but desperately needs all the income it can obtain this year.

So every one should arrive at a clear understanding of what he hopes to accomplish with his capital. Is it to be a source of retirement income 10 or 20 years hence or is it to carry the main burden of paying today's bills? Between these two extremes lies a whole spectrum of investment objectives.

The next step is to choose the best means of reaching one's goal. In narrowing the field of selection, the investor should carefully weigh the pros and cons of high-grade stocks versus fixed-income securities for his particular needs—present and future. His age, tax bracket, living style, estate plan, and temperament must all be taken into account.

In thinking about which stocks to own, he should recognize that the nature of individual companies varies greatly. For example, some have stable but below-average prospects and a high dividend payout. Others offer moderate growth and an average yield. Still others provide a strong earnings potential and a low current return.

A key consideration in selecting stocks today is their inflation-resistant characteristics. Many firms simply cannot raise their prices or improve their efficiency enough to offset their spiraling taxes, wages and other costs. As pay levels continue to climb steeply—and recent three-year settlements make it certain they will —a growing number of companies will be unable to make satisfactory earnings and dividend progress.

The crux of the matter is that while inflation does nobody any good, some firms are hurt less by it than others. The key factors behind the ability of a company or business to cope with inflation are:

1. Strong Growth of Demand
2. Low Labor Costs
3. Below-Average Capital Needs
4. Flexible Pricing Structure

Pricing flexibility is the most important of these considerations. Naturally, only a few types of businesses can score well on all points and qualitative factors must be considered as well. Subject to this proviso, following is a list of some of the industries which we rank as average or above-average in terms of their overall inflation-resistant characteristics:

Personal Care
Soft Drink
Business Services
Photographic
Food Processing
Drug

Office Equipment
General Merchandise Retail
Life Insurance
Machinery
Auto
Bank
Building Materials
Chemicals
Electrical Equipment
Petroleum

The individual companies selected should have strong finances. Their working capital has to be large enough to meet their present and near-term needs and they should not be overburdened with expensive debt. It is best if they are able to finance most of their expansion from their internally generated cash flow rather than from the frequent sale of debt instruments, convertible securities or common stock.

The firms should also have a leading position in their industry or markets. Whether they are large or small, they must be favorably situated relative to their competitors vis-a-vis costs, pricing, product or service uniqueness, marketing ability, etc. In short they should have proven success in their fields rather than being "special situations," "turn-around candidates" or of interest primarily for other transitory reasons.

In addition, the factor of investment quality must be carefully taken into account. Quality is basically the assessment of the risks involved both as to the under-lying company and the seasoning, marketability and valuation of the shares themselves. Ignoring quality is one of the biggest pitfalls of investing.

There are, of course, other considerations. The in-vestor must set up an overall diversification goal to-wards which to work. This schedule should give realistic weighting to the most favorably situated areas of the economy relative to his needs and objective. He should then buy only those stocks which "make sense" as far as his own program is concerned.

Conversely, the investor should not be swayed into buying issues that are off the beaten path and do not fit into his long-range goal. He must always be on his guard to resist the "smart money" talk that is all the rage when the stock market is booming.

Just as importantly, he should not panic during

bear markets and sell out his holdings. One of the
great advantages of owning the stocks of successful
companies is that, when the going gets rough, the
only people left to buy stocks are the true investors
who—then as always—are interested solely in the
top-quality issues. At the market lows, there is almost
nobody around to roll dice and buy the shares of
marginal companies.

The experienced investor who has been through
bear markets before *knows* that the high-grade stocks
will be the first to recover and to continue their long-
range progress. For this reason, he does not look upon
a drop in the price of a good stock as a *catastrophe*
but as an *opportunity* to buy more. In contrast, at
such times the owner of doggy issues usually becomes
frightened and either sells out right at the bottom
or as soon as he can recover a small part of his huge
loss.

The investor should continue to invest his surplus
income as it becomes available—if possible, as regularly and periodically as he pays his insurance premiums. By so doing, he will be continually building
up his portfolio's base and he will be much less likely
to become sidetracked from his goal by the continuous
shifts of market psychology.

Sticking to his long-range program will prevent him
from making another common type of error—selling a
suitable stock in his program because its earnings experience a quarterly drop or because it runs into one
of the slow periods that occur even for the best-man-
aged companies. Having a plan gives him the patience
to hold on to the right stocks even during their recur-
ring periods of unpopularity.

Building up a sound, well-balanced portfolio that
fits the investor's needs and objectives seems like a
simple task. Actually, it is quite difficult. It requires
great self-discipline to continue with the program
originally laid down, and it calls for a more cold-
blooded and unemotional attitude towards one's capital than most people possess.

In conclusion, the investor who is following a sensible long-range plan is basing his approach on holding
a part-ownership in companies which should benefit
the most from the economy's future progress. This is

a *proven* strategy which is *certain* to produce *good* results over his investment lifetime.*

The Monthly Investment Plan. At the outset of your investment plan, you may be able to afford only a small regular investment. Even that is a beginning, and you can do it with no more than $40 every three months. The Monthly Investment Plan of the New York Stock Exchange provides the opportunity. It's an easy, convenient way to save.

Once you're enrolled, you simply send in your payment regularly, monthly or quarterly. Your account is credited for full and fractional shares of stock you buy, less commission costs. You can pick any one of the 1,200 different securities on the NYSE, either the same one regularly or a different one each time. Dividends may be automatically reinvested.

Just be sure you've taken care of living expenses and have money set aside to meet emergencies first, even for this kind of investment plan. Write to the office of any member firm of the NYSE and ask for their booklet "How To Invest on a Budget—the Monthly Investment Plan."

It's a chance to be a part owner in big business, even in a small way, of General Motors, American Telephone and Telegraph, General Food, and a whole host of other companies. It's a sensible way to invest.

Dollar-cost averaging. Let's look at what happens when you invest the same dollar amount at regular intervals regardless of stock price fluctuations. If you practice dollar-cost averaging, such as with the Monthly Investment Plan, then when prices are high you will purchase fewer shares; when prices are low you'll get more shares for the same dollars. On the average, the cost of all shares you have purchased will be less than the average of the shares' prices.

Specifically, here's what happens to the shares you buy in dollar-cost averaging.

The key to this kind of program is your ability and determination to keep making regular purchases when prices are

---

* Reprinted with permission, the David L. Babson Investment Company, Inc., One Boston Place, Boston, Mass. 02108. August 20, 1970 Weekly Staff Letter.

down. Low prices are a sign to reduce your average costs. You get more shares for the same amount of money.

Of course, a dollar-cost averaging program will not guarantee a profit. It only guarantees an average cost to you of less than the average price of the shares. Mutual funds provide this kind of investing opportunity in a variety of companies, as does the MIP.

It's a good method to use for investing if you want to do so regularly at the least possible average cost per share.

Purchase Date	Amount Invested	Price per Share	Shares Purchased
Jan. 1	$ 100	$ 50	2.000
Feb. 1	100	60	1.667
Mar. 1	100	70	1.428
Apr. 1	100	80	1.250
May 1	100	90	1.111
June 1	100	100	1.000
July 1	100	80	1.250
Aug. 1	100	60	1.667
Sept. 1	100	50	2.000
Oct. 1	100	40	2.500
Nov. 1	100	30	3.333
Dec. 1	100	50	2.000
	$1,200	$760	21.206

Total amount invested	$ 1,200
Total shares purchased	21.206
Average price per share (Total price per share column $760 divided by 12)	$ 63.33
Average cost to investor (Amount invested $1,200 divided by shares purchased 21.206)	$ 56.58

Retirement Planning—Now
8

Planning for retirement begins now, not when you hit sixty-five. No matter how young you are, it is during your working years that you are accumulating the assets that will finance your expenses when you retire and are no longer working or earning a salary.

You may consider the enormous expenses of the present to be so burdensome that you put aside all thought of tomorrow. Yet, unless you do some planning now, you'll end up worse than ever when tomorrow comes.

Even clergymen must plan for their later years. We believe the Lord will take care of us, but he normally won't be able to unless we help along the way. You may have known many a minister who faithfully served his congregations through the years, living in church-owned homes, always at the minimum salary, getting by because members gave food and other useful items, but who, upon retiring, had nothing, and being destitute was entirely at the mercy of others for help.

It's not a pretty picture, nor an infrequent one. However, the likelihood of your retiring without any benefits or assets at all is far less than in previous decades. Clergymen are being forced into making financial provisions for their retirement,

whether they want to or not. Not only does Social Security
force such planning, but even denominational pension boards
have developed programs which literally force a clergyman
to save toward retirement.

For many clergymen, therefore, the combination of Social
Security, their own denominational pension plán, and perhaps a supplemental insurance plan offer the possibility of
far more retirement income than could have been expected
by a previous generation of ministers.

This chapter is intended to help you plan intelligently,
now, for your retirement. It should help you to achieve your
financial objectives for age sixty-five and beyond.

A recent survey aimed at determining the attitudes of
ministers who are approaching retirement age (between the
ages of sixty and sixty-four) towards financial planning for
retirement revealed that:

> The majority of Protestant member ministers of
> pre-retirement age are looking forward to retirement
> because they are ready for it, they won't have so much
> pressure, and there are things they want to do. How-
> ever, a sizeable minority have mixed emotions or are
> neutral towards retirement, and a minority don't want
> to retire.
>
> Similarly, the majority of ministers' wives are en-
> thused about retirement, but a sizeable minority are
> neutral or unenthused.
>
> Six out of ten Protestant member ministers of pre-
> retirement age would like to travel after retirement,
> but only four out of ten plan to do so. A majority do
> plan to be active in church affairs, one out of three
> plan to write, half plan to study, eight out of ten plan
> to pursue hobbies, and seven out of ten plan to be
> active in community affairs.
>
> Two out of three of these ministers plan on moving
> after they retire, primarily because their present
> housing is owned by the church.
>
> Almost all of these ministers will receive Social
> Security, most will receive a pension, about half will
> use savings, and a third will use life insurance as
> sources of retirement income.
>
> Half of these ministers say their income after retire-

ment will we "just enough," but one out of four say it will be "not quite enough." Inflation and the rise in the cost of living has already affected the planned income needed for retirement, and if inflation continues, half say their retirement income will be "less than adequate." *

This all suggests that clergymen are generally ready to retire at age sixty-five. Many of them now realize, too late perhaps, that their retirement income will simply not be adequate to meet even their minimal needs. Early financial planning can avoid much of the problem at age sixty-five.

Retirement income planning and your insurance program are invariably tied together. This is particularly true where your policies are accumulating cash value. Since you'll probably no longer need the coverage when you retire, those cash benefits are there for you to use for investment or living expenses.

Your insurance program should be geared to the amount of income you or your family might need if you died, were disabled, or retired. Thus, financial retirement planning is the business of developing a plan that will generate the income you will need in retirement.

That income need, of course, will be considerably less than it is prior to age sixty-five. Your children will be on their own and there will only be the two of you to support. For most people, their houses will be paid for. For the clergyman, who has been using a church-owned home during his entire career, that is one of the most difficult problems. Nevertheless, with proper planning the burden can be eased.

Tax-wise, you will have a double exemption at age sixty-five (currently $1,500 rather than $750), and the same for your spouse at that age. Your medical expenses may, however, be higher, and thus may offset that tax advantage (but with Medicare, that expense is not as much a factor as before).

A clergyman generally has about four possible sources of

* A Summary Report "Ministers Look Ahead to Retirement" June 30, 1972. Ministers' Life and Casualty Union, Minneapolis, Minnesota. Used with permission.

retirement income—Social Security, denominational (or commercial) pension plan, insurance, and savings. While benefits from the first two may be largely determined for you (thus you begin with that as an income base), you will determine how much insurance and savings you want to accumulate.

Now that most clergymen are covered by Social Security, this benefit can be anticipated rather precisely. Benefits may be increasing rather dramatically over the next several years. The chart of benefits noted on page 115 will suggest the retirement income you could expect with today's dollar value.

Your own denominational or private pension plan will provide certain income benefits to you also. An inquiry will get you an estimate of what you can expect based on your previous accumulations and assuming you continue at your present rate of premium payment.

Your insurance program will offer retirement income, too, depending on what kind of policies you have, and the options you may select at age sixty-five. Whatever you are able or willing to put into a savings account will offer that much additional asset value, dividends and interest income at retirement.

To begin your planning process you must determine how much retirement income you'll need, and what you can expect from existing programs and assets. You'll need an inventory of your retirement benefits. Estimates, of course, will have to do. Fill in the suggested form.

	Monthly income
Social Security benefits	$_____
Church or private pension plan	_____
Insurance & annuities	_____
Total	$_____
Estimated amount needed	_____
Difference	$_____

A negative difference will suggest the amount of savings and investments you will need to accumulate in order to have the income required at age sixty-five. At a 4 percent or 5 percent annual return, you can quickly calculate the amount of principal you'll need to generate the additional amount of income you think you'll need.

This table gives examples of higher Social Security benefits payable as a result of a 20 percent increase recently signed into law. As a result of the increase, the average monthly check for a retired worker rises from $129 to $156, and the average monthly check for a retired couple rises from $224 to $271. For a disabled worker, the average check rises from $144 to $173.

Average yearly earnings after 1950*	$923 or less	$ 3,000	$ 4,200	$ 5,400	$ 6,600	$ 7,800	$ 9,000
Retired worker 65 or older Disabled worker under 65	$ 84.50	$174.80	$213.30	$250.60	$288.40	$331.00	$354.50
Wife 65 or older	42.30	87.40	106.70	125.30	144.20	165.50	177.30
Retired worker at 62	67.60	139.90	170.70	200.50	230.80	264.80	283.60
Wife at 62, no child	31.80	65.60	80.10	94.00	108.20	124.20	133.00
Widow at 60	73.30	125.10	152.60	179.30	206.30	236.70	253.50
Widow or widower at 62	84.50	144.30	176.00	206.80	238.00	273.10	292.50
Disabled widow at 50	51.30	87.50	106.80	125.50	144.30	165.60	177.30
Wife under 65 and one child	42.30	92.50	157.40	217.30	233.90	248.30	265.90
Widowed mother and one child	126.80	262.20	320.00	376.60	432.60	496.60	531.80
Widowed mother and two children	126.80	267.30	370.70	467.90	522.30	579.30	620.40
One child of retired or disabled worker	42.30	87.40	106.70	125.30	144.20	165.50	177.30
One surviving child	84.50	131.10	160.00	188.00	216.30	248.30	265.90
Maximum family payment	126.80	267.30	370.70	467.90	522.30	579.30	620.40

* Generally, average earnings covered by Social Security are figured from 1951 until the worker reaches retirement age, becomes disabled, or dies. The maximum benefit for a retired worker in 1972 is $259.40 a month, based on average yearly earnings of $5,652. The higher benefits shown in the chart, based on average earnings shown in the columns on the right, generally will not be payable until later.

It is precisely that last item that could make the difference between a reasonably financially worry-free retirement or a very difficult time. Now is the time to begin the necessary accumulation of assets to be certain the income is available when needed. That is why your spending—savings plan is such an important part of that plan. If you are going to have the income you need in retirement, you cannot wait until age sixty-five to put the package together.

Consider the following hypothetical case.

The Reverend Ted Jones and his wife Jane (both age forty-two) have four children, ages ten, thirteen, sixteen, twenty. If Ted should die, he wants to be certain his family has at least $800 a month income, although that could decrease by about $200 when his youngest child has completed college eleven years hence. At that time Jane would probably be able to supplement her income by her own employment.

In addition, Ted would want a lump-sum payment of $18,000 to purchase a home for his family since he lives in a parsonage now. (If he owned his home now, that same payment could be used to pay any existing mortgage.) He also anticipates a need for $2,000 for final expenses and would like to set up a $3,000 emergency savings fund for his family. He expects it will take a minimum of approximately $10,000 to pay for the rest of his children's college education. It could take more, of course, but scholarships at his church college and lower tuition at state schools, summer jobs, plus living at home, should be sufficient.

On the other hand, if Ted lived to retirement age, he would like to have $600 a month for himself and his wife, or at least $500 a month for the survivor.

Thus, he estimates his needs this way:

	Required monthly income
For his family for the next eleven years	$ 800
For his wife after that and to her age sixty	$ 600
In retirement, for himself or his wife	$ 500
In retirement for himself and his wife	$ 600
Lump-sum payment required at his death before retirement:	
Home (or mortgage)	$ 18,000

Final expenses	2,000
Savings emergency fund	3,000
College expenses	10,000
	$33,000

Retirement planning is the task of financing those goals. Here is a possible procedure.

If Ted has been in Social Security for the required quarters to get full coverage and has been paying the maximum tax, then his family would receive maximum benefits. As his children reached eighteen (or until twenty-two if full-time college students), the monthly payments to them and his widow would diminish to a time when she would receive nothing, until she reached age sixty-five when she would get her widow's portion.

In Ted's case, his wife will be forty-nine when their youngest child is eighteen. From then until her age sixty she would receive nothing from Social Security. Under present legislation, Ted's family could receive about $400 a month for those first eight years, approximately $340 for the next two years after that, and about $170 for the following three years. At age sixty his widow would again begin receiving a payment, this time of approximately $120 a month for the rest of her life. If Ted lives to retirement at age sixty-five, his Social Security benefits will exceed $400 a month at today's dollar value.

In addition, Ted's widow could expect income from the church's pension plan, and from whatever insurance and savings may have been accumulated by Ted.

Upon inquiry at the appropriate denominational office, Ted is told that based on his present accumulation of contributions, his family would receive about $150 a month for the rest of Jane's life. He is told, also, that if his payments into the plan continue at the same rate, his accumulation at age sixty-five will be sufficient to provide a retirement income of about $200 a month.

Ted already has $18,000 of term life insurance and another

$10,000 of whole life. These policies will provide the required lump-sum payments at his death, at least until his youngest child is over twenty-one. By retirement age, the term policy will have expired and the whole life policy may generate about $50 a month for the rest of Ted's life or Jane's.

This then is what Ted now has in case of Ted's death at age forty-two:

Needs—	
Cash	$33,000
Income: 11 years (average)	$ 800/month
balance	$ 600/month
Available—	
Insurance policies	$28,000
Social Security: 8 years	$ 400/month
next 2 years	$ 340/month
next 3 years	$ 170/month
Jane, age 60	$ 120/month
Church pension	$ 150/month

Ted needs approximately $250 a month more income to meet his goals. A $30,000 decreasing twenty-year term policy would generate that income now, and a lesser amount each year as the end of the term approached. That would cost Ted about $250 a year in premiums.

On the other hand, in case Ted retired at age sixty-five:

Needs—	
Income: for Ted and Jane	$ 600/month
Available—	
Social Security	$ 400/month
Church pension	$ 200/month
Insurance	$ 50/month
	$ 650/month

Ted's needs will apparently be met without the purchase of additional insurance for retirement income.

Your insurance and retirement needs, of course, will be different from Pastor Jones and his wife's. But this, at least, is the kind of financial planning you ought to be doing to be certain you and your family know what to expect. Your church pension-plan officials or the officers of a private plan will be most helpful. A good insurance agent (C.L.U.) can also be helpful.

Retirement housing. Retirement income is only one feature of your retirement plan. Now, before you reach age sixty-five, is the time to consider other matters, too. Perhaps most important is the matter of housing.

Referring again to the recent survey on "Ministers Look Ahead to Retirement," it is reported that:

> Two out of three of the ministers say they plan to move after they retire. The great majority of these say they will move because they now live in a parsonage or manse or house that belongs to a church. About one out of five say they plan to stay in their present house or apartment, and the others do not know or do not plan to retire.
>
> Half of the Protestant member ministers who are approaching retirement age say that they plan to move to a different community after they retire. One out of seven say that they plan to do so because they don't believe a minister should retire where he has served, and one out of eight said that they own a home or property elsewhere.
>
> Less than one out of ten say they plan to stay in the same community after they retire, one out of five don't know or are not sure what they will do, and one out of five plan to stay in their same home.
>
> A majority of those who plan to move to a different community have made some preparations, such as owning a home there or knowing the area well or having looked for housing there. About one out of three of those who plan to move to a different community have made no preparation for the move.

So much uncertainty about retirement housing suggests that clergymen have not done much planning on circumstances for their retirement. As important as housing is for everyone, clergymen must give serious thought to the matter, or as so many before them have experienced, retirement will be a traumatic and financially impossible task.

If anything speaks against the use of a parsonage, manse, or church-owned house it is precisely this. A clergyman, under those circumstances for all of his life, simply has no equity in any other house. He has actually been renting all his life, and like any renter he has nothing to show for all his costs. Of course, he did have a roof over his head during that time, and he may have had a far more elegant and comfortable home than he could have possibly afforded for himself. Nevertheless, when he can no longer serve a church (or when his wife is left without him), he has nowhere to go.

In all fairness to the profession, clergymen should be given an opportunity to purchase their own homes, even if it means buying and selling several homes in the course of a lifetime and through several pastorates. During all that time there will be a tendency to build up a certain amount of equity that by retirement may be sufficient to pay for a home without debt at age sixty-five.

Thus, the clergyman who can buy his own home will actually be planning for his retirement. Of course, where he finally buys his last home and lives during retirement is another matter. His choices there will be the same as most other retired persons. He will have to decide whether to live in a community in which he has served as pastor, or in some other place.

The clergyman who uses a church-owned home must make alternate plans, and he'd best do so as early in life as he can. One church official has suggested that congregations who furnish a home should fund an extra $300 or $400 each year for their pastor so he can build some equity.

"Your pastor is paying for your parsonage because you reduce his salary to meet the mortgage payments," he tells them. "That's immoral and unfair. Give your pastor a break. Face up to his needs. Be sure, one way or the other, that he gets the equity he'll someday need and has in fact earned." An annual funding, at each congregation served, can, in a lifetime, provide the nest egg necessary for at least partial payment on a house and lot, if not the whole cost.

Other than that, the only way you can build up an equity is to budget regular savings that will accumulate. Investments in stocks and real estate that tend to increase in value help to generate a larger sum than simply paying into a savings account. Such planning, however, does not remove the financial disadvantages of a parsonage, but is certainly necessary if that handicap to your retirement housing is to be overcome.

More retirement planning. As you look ahead to retirement, you need to be concerned with more than just income and housing, although these loom as the two most important items, at least financially. Many of your decisions hinge upon these two, or at least affect them.

You also need to decide what it is you are going to do in retirement. You'll want to do something, maybe you'll keep preaching, at least on a part-time basis, and perhaps at different locations on Sunday. Maybe you won't preach any more at all. You could write, travel, or just plan to be useful somehow.

In the survey referred to previously, about four out of ten ministers replied, when asked what they planned to do when they retire, that they plan to travel; about four out of ten say they plan to continue in the ministry part time; and almost one out of six say they plan to continue to be useful.

And, continues the summary statement of that report, "more than two out of three Protestant ministers who are approaching retirement said that they do plan to be active after they retire. Almost half of these ministers said that they could not quit because it's been their life's work, and nearly as many said that they plan to be active, not full-time, but to help where and when needed."

No doubt you, too, will find a variety of interesting activities that will keep you busy, useful, and happy, but you must plan for them now.

The type of housing you'll want in retirement will affect the way you live, too. Right now you may have a comfortable, large, suburban house. Is that the most practical for your retirement? Perhaps a smaller home is better. Should you move into an apartment, a home, or live with others? Your health at retirement will decide some of these questions for you, but you need to look forward to what fits your needs and desires best, given the health and attitude you expect to have at sixty-five.

Retirement living will normally cost less than now. Where you live, of course, affects your expenses since it obviously costs more in some places than others. A cost-of-living index by cities will quickly convince you of that. It's much less expensive to live in Austin, Texas, Durham, North Carolina, or Atlanta than in Hartford, Connecticut or Buffalo, New York, or San Francisco. If you have managed to get a home paid for, you won't have mortgage payments to worry about anymore.

Furthermore, you won't be paying Social Security taxes or making contributions to your pension plan anymore once you're retired. Your income taxes will be less. You'll drive your car much less, and you'll need only one car instead of the two you may have had before. You don't have as many other professional expenses either—certificates, clerical clothes, books, subscriptions, and the like.

In retirement you'll spend less for clothing, and maybe less on food. You will probably discontinue any payments to a savings plan, and your life insurance premiums may stop, too. On the other hand, your medical costs may go up, and if you travel you'll be spending more on recreation. Whatever your expenses, you'll put together your spending plan as described in an earlier chapter. It's just that the items you include are different at age sixty-five than they were at age forty.

In addition, then, to your retirement income, investments, housing, and what you plan to do when you retire, don't overlook your last will and testament. It's a very important document for your survivors, and should be part of your annual personal financial review. Your will should be updated frequently. Don't assume things will just take care of themselves. Have a will now and keep it up-to-date, even after you retire.

Professional counseling may be useful as you anticipate retirement. Your church headquarters, especially your pension board, can steer you in the right direction. The Retirement Advisors' Organization, 4 West 57th Street, N.Y. 10019, has a number of helpful booklets as well as a monthly publication that offer a lot of hints on successful retirement plans. The American Association of Retired Persons, 215 Long Beach Blvd., Long Beach, Calif. 90801 provides additional helps to retirees. The federal government's numerous publications offer the retiree even more assistance. Try "A Guide to Budgeting for the Retired Couple." It'll help you plan the financial part of your retirement plan.

Most important, though, begin planning now. Search out all the materials you can to help you make a smooth and orderly transition from an active parish leadership role to a more leisurely, less pressured role in retirement. Plan now for then. When the time comes, you'll be glad you did.

Bibliography

Banker, John C. *Personal Finance for Ministers*. Philadelphia: The Westminster Press, 1968.

Bramer, John. *Personal Finance for Clergymen*. Englewood Cliffs, N.J.: Prentice-Hall, 1964.

Changing Times, The Kiplinger Magazine. Editors Park, Md.: The Kiplinger Washington Editors, Inc.

Ernst and Ernst. *Clergy's Federal Income Tax Guide*. Nashville: Abingdon Press, annual.

Gray, Gary M., and Mitchell, Allen D. *The Prophet's Dollar*. New York: Exposition Press, 1971.

Holck, Manfred. *A Better Pay Package, The Minister's Housing Allowance, The Minister's Income Tax*, cassette tapes. Minneapolis: Minister's Life Resources.

_____, editor. *Church and Clergy Finance*. The bi-weekly financial newsletter for clergy. Minneapolis: Minister's Life Resources.

_____. *Money Management for Ministers*. Minneapolis: Augsburg Publishing House, 1966.

Hungerford, Kenneth G. *Federal Income Tax Handbook for Clergy*. Wilmington, Del.: Associated Publishers, annual.

Joslin, G. S. *The Minister's Law Handbook*. Manhasset, N.Y.: Channel Press, 1962.

125

Lasser, J. K. *Your Income Tax.* New York: Simon & Schuster, annual.

Markstein, David L. *Manage Your Money and Live Better.* New York: McGraw-Hill Book Co., 1971.

Planning Your Financial Future. Washington, D.C.: U.S. News and World Report Money Management Library, 1972.

Smith, Carlton, and Pratt, Richard Putnam. *The Time-Life Book of Family Finance.* New York: Time-Life Books, 1969.

Unger, Maurice A., and Wolf, Harold A. *Personal Finance.* Third Edition. Boston: Allyn & Bacon, 1972.

Your Federal Income Tax, Washington, D.C.: U.S. Government Printing Office, annual.

Wiltsee, Joseph L. *Business Week's Guide to Personal Business.* New York: McGraw-Hill Book Co., 1970.

How to Live on Your Income. New York: Reader's Digest, 1970.